Pastor Karl's Rookie Year

KARL BECK

Twelve Unexpected Truths About Church Life

Illustrations by
Kevin Pope

INTERVARSITY PRESS
DOWNERS GROVE, ILLINOIS 60515

The first twelve chapters in this book were adapted from essays originally published in The Door.

Illustrations ©1993 by Kevin Pope

InterVarsity Press® is the book-publishing division of InterVarsity Christian Fellowship®, a student movement active on campus at hundreds of universities, colleges and schools of nursing in the United States of America, and a member movement of the International Fellowship of Evangelical Students. For information about local and regional activities, write Public Relations Dept., InterVarsity Christian Fellowship, 6400 Schroeder Rd., P.O. Box 7895, Madison, WI 53707-7895.

All Scripture quotations, unless otherwise indicated, are from the HOLY BIBLE, NEW INTERNATIONAL VERSION®. NIV®. Copyright© 1973, 1978, 1984 by International Bible Society. Used by permission of Zondervan Publishing House. All rights reserved.

Cover illustration: Kevin Pope

ISBN 0-8308-1835-9

Printed in the United States of America

Library of Congress Cataloging-in-Publication Data

Beck, Karl, d. 1991.
    Pastor Karl's rookie year: twelve unexpected truths about church
life/Karl Beck.
      p.   cm.
    ISBN 0-8308-1835-9
    1. Christian life—1960-   2. Clergymen's writings. I. Title.
    BV4501.2.B3885   1993
    253—dc20   92-42470
                                          CIP

17	16	15	14	13	12	11	10	9	8	7	6	5	4	3	2	1
06	05	04	03	02	01	00	99	98	97	96	95	94	93			

The Story Behind Pastor Karl 7

Pastor Karl Strikes Out (Sort Of) 11
Truth #1: Churches will accept ordinary, fallible
human beings behind the pulpit.

Corrie ten Boom Doesn't Let Us off the Hook 23
Truth #2: Heroes in the faith aren't supposed to
give us an excuse for avoiding our own discipleship.

In Defense of Senior Saints 31
Truth #3: Despite what you've been told, the old
people in the congregation are really among its
most valuable and forward-looking members.

Counseling Your Average Moral Hyena 39
Truth #4: People not only know they're sinful—
they think they're *uniquely* awful.

Never Trust a Spiritual Revolution You Can't Dance To 45
Truth #5: The real problem with the New Age
movement is that it tries to make us think we can
control our fate.

The Prophet Edgar (and Other Unlikely Heroes) 53
Truth #6: Terms defined in seminary take on
new meaning in the local church.

87925

A Worthy Adversary Relinquishes His Chainsaw   *63*
Truth #7: Chaperoning youth retreats is never
as bad as people say—it's worse.

Paul Plants, Apollos Waters, Karl Frets   *73*
Truth #8: You can't measure success in the church,
but maybe it doesn't hurt to try.

Paint Boldly—and Trust God   *81*
Truth #9: Don't try to evangelize with art; don't
try to make evangelism into great art.

How to Keep Discipleship from Dying   *89*
Truth #10: You choose a church like you choose
a spouse—it's a long-term commitment.

The Great Color-Scheme Schism   *97*
Truth #11: At your average church, it's easier
to introduce a fourth person into the Trinity
than to introduce a new carpet pattern into the
nave.

Why Preaching Will Never Be an Olympic Event   *105*
Truth #12: Sermons aren't supposed to be enduring
literary contributions, just Dixie cups bearing living
water to parched people.

Happy Birthday to Jesus, Happy Birthday to Us   *111*
A Christmas Sermon

The Story Behind Pastor Karl

Life in the church is, in many ways, like life in a marriage. It's never exactly what you thought it was going to be before you got into it. A good marriage counselor can prepare you for a lot of things, but the full reality of marriage is known only *in* marriage. Likewise, a strong seminary education can prepare someone for the ministry, but actually being a minister is a lot different from thinking or dreaming about it. That's what Karl Beck found out in his rookie year behind the pulpit.

This book is about the surprising things—both painful and pleasurable—that can be learned only through working in the church. Though Pastor Karl Beck and his Zion Community Church are fictional creations, they are based on real-life persons and incidents. Pastor Karl is a keen-eyed, feisty, witty, occasionally caustic but always self-critical cleric. Presented here, through his persona, is a series of wry truths that will help any Christian—ordained or lay—better understand and appreciate life in the Christian community.

Pastor Karl is the invention of Charles B. Westerman (referred to by those who knew him simply as "Chuck"), who indeed was in a situation close to Karl's. Chuck was a recent graduate of Northern Baptist Theological Seminary (Lombard, Illinois), undertaking his initial pastorate at Calvary Baptist Church in Cheyenne, Wyoming, when he began writing as Karl Beck in *The Door*. In 1990 he was diagnosed with a brain tumor. He died in 1991. The pages that follow include all his Karl Beck stories and commentary, as well as an insightful sermon that Karl himself, we can trust, might well have preached.

The Editors

1
Pastor Karl Strikes Out (Sort Of)

Truth #1: Churches will accept ordinary, fallible human beings behind the pulpit.

I n the course of the past summer, I've discovered why I entered the ministry, and what kind of minister I am.

First, the former discovery, which will help explain the latter.

I didn't, I've found, become a pastor because I wanted to be one ever since I was a little boy. I didn't become a pastor because I wanted to emulate some role-model pulpiteer of my youth. I didn't follow in any family footsteps.

I didn't become a pastor out of any sober assessment of my gifts and inclinations. Professional Christian service didn't even show up on one of those vocational printouts you get after filling in the answers to questions ("Would you rather spend your time [a] taking apart a catalytic converter; [b] reading the works of Emily Dickinson; [c] frying insects under a magnifying glass") with a sharpened number-2 pencil on a computer worksheet under the benevolent gaze of a high-school guidance counselor. And I never received any divine command to preach the Word in a stifling sunset vision on the last night at a church summer camp.

I realized this summer that the reason I became a pastor was that (a) most churches have softball teams and (b) if you're the minister of the church, they definitely have to let you play, and probably have to let you start.

Gee. That almost makes me sound shallow.

What you must understand, though, is that for all my jockish inclinations, baseball (along with its gentler counterpart, softball) is the one sport I've never mastered. It is also the one sport I love with a grand passion.

Among my extended family I can count real Bull Durhams—actual minor leaguers, which is to say, actual minor gods. My grandfather played grade-school sandlot ball with Babe Ruth in Baltimore, and later scouted for John McGraw. I was born with a genetic love for the National Pastime and yet, alas, cruelly, with no genetic talent for the game.

And so I have plodded away in grade-school summer leagues and on college intramural squads, always eager, always knowledgeable, always riding the bench. The realization that ordination would finally get me into the game has been, I now recognize, a prime motivation behind my aspirations to the ministry. I donned a clerical robe with an unconscious wish to don, in logical sequence, a pin-striped team jersey.

And I have not been disappointed.

"Are you going to play, Pastor?" asked Ed Rodriguez as he taped the softball sign-up sheet to the sanctuary wall one Sunday after Easter.

Am I going to play? Heh, heh. Careful now. Be a bit coy. Don't seem too eager.

"Yeah. I might."

I held off penciling in my name for exactly forty-six seconds after Ed wandered off to pin on his usher's badge for the morning. I was in. I would participate.

And so I did. And in doing so, I discovered Who I Am as a person of the cloth.

It started innocently enough.

I was there, glove oiled, jersey (numeral "27" ironed on the front, "The Rev" stenciled neatly on the back) properly half-tucked in, popping the ball in my mitt, fiercely chomping away on half a pack of Major League Chew (the bubble gum, not the tobacco), psyched for the first practice on the broad green lawn of the public park around the block from the church.

The Tiger, The Kid, The Beast (I hoped my boundless enthusiasm would get me tagged with the latter nickname in time; maybe, biblical scruples aside, I could get my number changed to "666") had come to play, or at least to practice, ready to assume the crouch behind the plate, hot dog catcher for the Zion Community All-Stars.

So I was half an hour early. I shagged my own flies, OK? Eventually, the rest of the team drifted onto the field: Ed Rodriguez warming up his rainbow-arc pitching motion, George Alonzo popping out lazy flies with lots of chatter, Fred Armitage and his boy Lee limbering up to take the diamond as the slickest father-son double-play combination on the ecclesiastical circuit.

Yeah. It was a made-to-order sermon illustration on the meaning of heaven. As the evening proceeded, and evenings after it, we were welded into one sleek, mean softball machine.

I did myself proud in batting practice, dropping nasty little base hits into shallow left, beating out deep grounders, talking it up. I had a lock on the starting catcher's slot well before the first game. That we had a core of only nine regular players (ten, once Lonnie Lavelle's rotation at the firehouse ended) and looked like we would occasionally have to play without a short center fielder didn't diminish my pride any. I'd made the squad.

The first inkling that everything wasn't altogether copacetic came not on the playing field, but at a Sunday-evening potluck before the inauguration of a Tony Campolo video series in early May.

"Ready for the first game?" I asked Ed Rodriguez as I passed on the third in a sequence of green bean/mushroom soup/onion ring/sliced almond casseroles at the buffet table. "Wanna get together to work on your strike zone before Tuesday?"

Ed scooped a spoonful of frothy Jello-Something onto the side of his plate and demurred. "Uh. Naw. I think I'm ready."

"Yeah, you probably are." I poured myself a cup of Sanka.

"Uh, Karl . . ."

"Yo."

Ed and I headed to an open table and sat down. Ed murmured a short grace (I should've known something was up—I'd already blessed the food) and attacked a crust of French bread.

"You know, you seem pretty pepped up for this. I'd mmpf nr klgle, but . . ."

"Finish chewing."

"Sorry. Uh, look. I'm glad you're pumped to play, but I was thinking . . ."

"What? Spill it." Ed's a trustee. Probably wondering about the lawn-care contract.

"Well, you seem a little . . . um, intense in practice. Yeah.

Intense. Are you going to settle in OK?"

Hah. Nerves. He wasn't sure I'd be able to keep my composure in the heat of competition.

"No sweat," I replied. "I'm stoked for the opener, but I'll be able to, you know, follow the play."

"Oh, I'm not worried about that." He took a swig of lemonade. "You'll do fine. But some of the guys were thinking that you're maybe too serious about this."

"Serious?" Too serious? About softball? Too serious about softball? It was an oxymoron of sorts. "Serious how?"

"Well, like screaming at Bill Eldridge for missing the cutoff man the other night."

I reflected. "I wasn't screaming at him, Ed. Just reminding him. He'll get it right once we're playing."

"OK, but it wasn't the only time. I mean, you took Roger out at home plate in the scrimmage Friday. He's our oldest player, Karl. It was just intrasquad, six-on-six. You're hopping up and down all the time, calling guys off pop-ups like it's the last out of the seventh game of the World Series."

I obviously looked puzzled.

"Ah, I don't know. We'll have fun. Just have fun, Karl. We're just playing for fun."

"Fun? Ed, I'm having the time of my life."

* * *

First game against Manheim Lutheran, we're down six runs by the end of the second inning. I've blown a relay to home and popped up weakly in my first at-bat.

Composure. Composure. This isn't like practice. I'm so eager to get to Ed's pitches that I'm leaning in and I almost get my head taken off by a free-swinging batter. Finally, the burly Lutheran second baseman catches the tip of my mitt as he takes a cut at a ball outside the plate, and he gets first base on an interference call. I remonstrate gently with the umpire.

"Interference? Who's interfering with whom? I'm just trying to catch the pitch. That guy stepped out of the batter's box to go after it!"

"Chill out, Pastor. Next batter."

"But wait, wait. How can you say—"

"Oh, Karl!"

Ed is calling me out to the mound for a conference. I tell the umpire to hold on a second and I jog out to the pitching rubber. "Can you believe—"

"Chill out, Pastor."

"So I've been told."

"Just let the pitches come in to you. The ump's right. Calm down. We'll get back in this."

That's when I notice the rest of my teammates looking at each other and rolling their eyes.

"OK. OK."

I troop back behind the plate and pull down my catcher's mask. The next guy up dumps a single into right, then Ed walks the opposing shortstop on five pitches—the last one, I swear, right over the plate and belt-high. I'm a little miffed, I admit. "*Ball four?* That was a strike!"

The umpire smiles confidently. "I call 'em as I see 'em, Rev."

"Is that with or without your contacts in?"

A groan goes up across the field. I catch sight of my wife behind the backstop with her hand over her face. The ump's smile fades.

"We aren't questioning my professional acumen here, are we, Pastor?"

I grumble a bit more but, you know, it's in bounds, all part of the show. Bases loaded. Let's get on with it.

The next batter hangs back on two perfect pitches, both called balls. I'm steamed now, in an Old Testament sort of way—the righteous anger of Jehovah. I glare at the ump. The next pitch is a little inside, but the guy at the plate steps back and wallops it to the fence.

One run comes in, two, three, while George Alonzo chases down the ball and wings it back to the infield. The hitter is chugging around third, looking for an inside-the-park homer. The ball is traveling down the line.

"Don't cut it! Don't cut it!" I'm shouting at our third base-man and focusing on the incoming missile. I trap it in my glove and turn to put the tag on the runner.

Which I make.

Whatever other conclusions are drawn from this episode, let the record show that I *made the tag*. Third out. Our at-bat.

Only my friend in the blue shirt and chest protector chooses not to see it that way. He's hardly finished sweeping his arms out across his body when I'm on my feet, charging.

"I got him!" I yell.

"Safe!" he yells back.

"Safe? *Safe?* I nailed him two feet from the plate!"

That dang self-righteous smile again. "Well then, too bad I didn't have my contacts in then. The runner is safe." The ump turns his back, clicks his ball-and-strike counter back to 0-0, and bends down to brush off home plate.

This is too much, really. Ed heads toward me, motioning "calm"—but how can I, a minister of the gospel, be unimpassioned about such a blatant miscarriage of justice? I follow the umpire.

"So just what exactly would it take around here to get a guy out? You need photos next time? Blow-ups?"

"Next batter."

"Speaking. See, that was the third out, so *I'm the next batter,* chowderhead."

Ed, on his way to restraining me, pivots and heads back to the mound. Why waste the steps? Ed knows "over" when he hears it.

The ump resumes his smug smile. "But Pastor, there's no way you can be the next batter . . . because *you're outta the game!"*

Outta the . . . ? Outta . . . Then it dawns on me. Here I am, pastor, leader, role model for my flock. And I've just been ejected, in front of God and the Zion Community cheering section (unfortunately, a large one), from a friendly athletic competition for losing my cool and bad-mouthing a Community Recreation employee.

My credibility as a spiritual muckymuck, so carefully preserved through eight months of Sunday services and raucous board meetings, has just been blown over a couple bad calls on a ball diamond.

I slink off to my car (I could've walked under the chassis) with the sudden realization that I've just proved for all the world to see what kind of person and, more important, what kind of pastor I am.

I believe that in the ministry manuals it's called "a buffoon."

I'm sitting in the car with the wife and kids ("Mommy, the game's still going on. Why isn't Daddy playing anymore?"), my head on the steering wheel.

"A chowderhead. I called him a chowderhead."

"Well, yes dear, you did."

"I'm through. Through. They'll call a congregational meeting for Saturday, fire me officially on Sunday, and we're outta here.

Word will spread. No one else will take me. We'll starve. I'll
have to work at Sears. All because I'm a . . . I'm a—"

"A hypercompetitive jerk?"

Thank the Lord for a helpmeet who can supply just the right
phrase when one is speechless.

"I think you're a human being. God forbid that Zion Community Church should have one of *those* behind the pulpit.
Now turn the key, and maybe we can get to Dairy Queen before
it closes."

* * *

Turns out the church *will* accept "one of those"—a human
being—right behind the pulpit. Turns out that's exactly What
Kind of Minister I Am, and the congregation is tickled to have
it confirmed before witnesses. Turns out they suspected it all
along, way before I, with my self-induced visions of vocational
grandeur (why else would they call it *divinity* school?), had a
clue. Turns out that perfect comportment in all situations isn't
on my job description after all, and I'm the only one who ever
thought it was.

Lingering repercussions from my outburst? Well, my kids
have expanded their vocabulary. Before, when I got upset about
something at home, they would cower in a corner. Now they
bounce happily on the sofa cushions and chant, singsong: "Daddy's a hypercompetitive jerk, Daddy's a hypercompetitive jerk."

In addition, the pastor from Manheim Lutheran has had a
field day at Ministerial Association breakfasts. I can't walk into
the restaurant and slap one of my professional comrades on the
back now without him sidling up to me and saying, "Nice tag,"
or "You got 'im that time."

Oh, and one more thing. I do have a new nickname. The first
Sunday after the Big Game, Ed Rodriguez and the boys gath-

ered at the lectern during announcements and called me forward for a presentation. As I stepped sheepishly among them,
to the accompaniment of congregational titters, they reached
under the pulpit and hauled out a brand-new softball jersey.
They held it up for all to see, front and back, and handed it to
me amidst cheers and applause.

Ironed on the front was the numeral "0." Stenciled neatly
across the back were the words "Pastor Chowderhead."

2
Corrie ten Boom Doesn't Let Us off the Hook

Truth #2: Heroes in the faith aren't supposed to give us an excuse for avoiding our own discipleship.

Most preachers wouldn't touch the Ananias and Sapphira episode with a ten-foot pledge card. It's not that the story isn't effective. Heavens, the easy moral alone—"Turn over all your recent capital gains to the church or you're maggot entree"—could serve as the infrastructure for a decade's worth of stewardship campaigns.

But that's the problem. We ministers like to think that we approach the question of appropriately motivated giving with discretion and finesse. Compared to the New Testament account of Old Testament retribution found in Acts 5:1-11, *The Texas Chainsaw Massacre* is an industrial training film on the safe use of power tools. "Give till it hurts" indeed.

And yet perhaps the time for subtlety—not to say squeamishness—regarding some of the harder scriptural lessons on material and personal sacrifice is over.

We all have our pet anecdotes on self-serving "Christian service." I personally cherish the one about the suburban church
that stopped sending Christmas gifts to a children's group on
a tribal reservation because "we never got any thank-you notes
back" (ungrateful little Injuns!). And then there's the mother
who called an inner-city agency asking if she could bring her
children into town to see some poor people "so my kids will be
grateful for all the things they have." ("Zoo tours queue to the
right—'Tropical Bird House' begins immediately; 'Object-Les-
son Indigents' leaves in fifteen minutes.")

But these are simply the grosser examples of a misguided
paternalism that will be with us always. In their wholesale na-
iveté, they approach the personification of what Catholic theo-
logians have always tagged "invincible ignorance."

What we seem to be dealing with nowadays is something
more virulent, a pious trend toward bogus compassion that bids
to become to the late twentieth century what folk masses and
clown ministries were to earlier epochs. (No, I'm not misusing
the term. In the fad-laden world of fin-de-siècle America, an
"epoch" has a shelf life of no more than half a decade.) Pocket-
change "adoptions" of Third World infants, the gracious dona-
tion of spare hours to a bank of phonathon hookups, participation in in-and-out educational tours to blighted locales and
other ostentatious conscience-assuaging maneuvers have come
to pass as "incarnational ministry" in Christendom today.

OK, I can already hear the anguished cries of relief agencies
and parachurch organizations across the country. "That spud-
head is cavalierly chipping away at our volunteer base! From
his lofty perch he's pooh-poohing the minimal but vital contributions that keep our doors open! Where does he get off knock-

ing fledgling attempts at service that may yet soar into sacrificial investments—and if they don't, so what? At least we crack the ministry nut this month and keep our phones connected and the heat on a little longer."

Anguished cries heard and acknowledged. I realize that deeply spiritual involvement in social problem-solving often results from what initially presents itself as mere casual contact. And I realize that every little bit helps. And now I'm supposed to say that I also realize that we can't all be Mother Teresas and Martin Luther Kings and Lech Walesas and Oscar Romeros and Corrie ten Booms and immolate ourselves in the crucible of divine love manifested as radical self-giving.

But I ain't gonna say that, because it ain't true. I'm not going to trot out the Honor Roll of Great Christians of Our Time for the same reason that it's usually trotted out, which is to make us feel all warm and gushy inside that someone on Our Religious Team is holding up the side while the most of us take care of Real World business. Mother Teresa et al. are not proxies, they're paradigms; nor, as has been noted elsewhere, are they particularly extraordinary disciples of Jesus Christ—they are average disciples who are made to look extraordinary by the sloth and complacency of most professed Christians. Why *can't* we all be Corrie ten Booms and Martin Luther Kings? Who excused any of us from trying to be?

Herein lies the real kernel of the story of Ananias and Sapphira, and its application to the sham clarity of the contemporary church. The pertinent issue, you see, never has been whether or to what extent one is willing to turn over one's energies and acquisitions to God. The issue is whether one is willing to turn oneself over to God, heart and soul, mind and strength, lock, stock and VISA account.

We have, you say? We're coming out of one of the greatest Christian revivals since the nineteenth century, you say? Look across America at all the lives that have been changed by Jesus Christ, you say?

I'm sorry. I don't believe conversion is measured by "changed lives." (Especially if the "changes" are the simple replacement of "worldly" predilections and customs by "Christian" ones: Steve Green for Kenny Loggins, prayer breakfasts for Rotary Club luncheons, "Praise the Lord, I hit my thumb with a hammer!" for "*!#*!, I hit my thumb with a hammer!" and ten dollars a week in the collection plate for ten dollars a week to United Way. This is not evidence of "changed lives," or even, for that matter, "changed tastes." It is sanctimonious substitutionism.) Conversion is measured by *uprooted* lives.

Simply put, what percentage of Christians do you see inconvenienced by their faith anymore? And no, I'm not talking about the "I tried to witness to the bag boy at Safeway this morning and he laughed at me" brand of costly discipleship so favored by persecution-complex evangelicals.

I'm talking about true inconvenience, dislocation on a discomfiting scale. If so many of us have given our lives to Jesus so that he can do with them what he wants, isn't it a little suspicious that so many of our lives don't look a groatsworth's different than they would have if we hadn't so given them? It forces one to posit either a lack of imagination on the Savior's part or a lack of response on ours. (Anyone care to take a stab at reducing those options?)

"Social problems won't be solved until hearts are transformed by the Holy Spirit." Isn't that our favorite verbal anodyne for challenges to the church's complacency in the face of cultural chaos?

OK, let's assume for the moment that it's true. Quick—who's the last person of your acquaintance who gave her life to Jesus Christ and promptly went out and blew her savings setting up a job-training program for urban youth? Or who sacrificed the vice-presidency of a marketing agency to do economic development in Haiti? Or who put his life at risk standing up to the friendly neighborhood drug cartel? Or who marched down to the local children's agency and brought home a passel of unadoptable kids, stopping on the way at the lawyer's office so guardianship papers could be drawn up? Or who launched without pause into an evangelism field she was uniquely connected to serve, without the backing of an established parachurch ministry that guaranteed financial support until the year 2011 or when Jesus returns, whichever comes first?

Can you imagine *any* of the seriously imbalanced characters who populate the book of Acts (sandwiching good old Ananias and Sapphira by the chapterful) blinking twice at any of these tasks? Can you imagine *anyone* of your religious acquaintance seriously considering the possibilities?

No, no, no, no. Cut the outraged sniveling. I'm not gainsaying that there are multitudes of unsung believers out there Brightening the Corner Where They Are, living quiet lives of spiritual heroism in the mundane circumstances of contemporary American existence. I'm not maintaining that the only valid evidence of grace in the average Christian experience is an immediate removal to a Third World hovel. I'm not advocating salvation via Grand Gesture as an antidote to salvation by token renunciation.

But I am questioning why so few grand gestures—legitimately inspired and rationally conceived or otherwise—are attempted as a matter of course by any of the tens of millions of professing believers who populate this nation. I am wondering why so few widows' mites find their way into the treasury. And I am curious why so many of us are closer in our sharing of ourselves to Ananias and Sapphira (don't these people have last names? "bar-Simeon"? "Antiochus"? "Johanssen"?) than we are to their immediate scriptural predecessor, Barnabas of Cyprus, who (Acts 4:36-37) "sold a field he owned and brought [all?!] the money and put it at the apostles' feet."

Our discipleship, the cliché has it, won't be graded on a curve. True enough. But the obverse of this observation (drawn as well from pedagogic jargon) is equally worth considering. Our discipleship evaluation *will* be competency-based. It *will* be normed to Jesus himself. And it *will* be judged pass/fail.

Ponder and act accordingly.

3
In Defense of Senior Saints

Truth #3: Despite what you've been told, the old people in the congregation are really among its most valuable and forward-looking members.

Beware of the patriarchs and matriarchs." This was the word we received in seminary, and no, it had nothing to do with the Old Testament midterm on the latter half of Genesis.

Rather, the warning's specific *Sitz im Leben* (bear with me— I don't get to do divinity-school jargon very much anymore) was our future entry into the world of the small "family" church to which most of us would be assigned upon graduation and ordination.

You see, professors of practical ministry take a perverse pleasure in painting for prospective preachers the potential pitfalls of pastoral practice. A favorite topic for classroom rumination is congregational power structures, and the accompanying horror stories that get told around the seminary campfire frequently involve ministers who walk all unawares into a fellowship guarded zealously and jealously by ancient "doorkeepers."

The elders (chronological, not ecclesiastical) in your classic Little Brown Church in the Subdivision, we are to believe, have been furnished by the Holy Spirit with the Gift of Troublemaking (not listed in 1 Corinthians 12, but quasi-scriptural nonetheless). This is their church, in a Panama-Canalish sort of sense: they built it, they paid for it, and they're going to keep it.

Anyone who challenges their authority in matters mundane (doctrine and polity) or essential (are the newcomers recognized at the beginning or the end of announcements? is it the Women's Mission League or the deaconesses who are responsible for keeping the kitchen tea canister filled?) gets sent through the Backbiting Windmill (Senior Circuit) for a first offense, and gets disfellowshipped or elected Chair of the Stewardship Campaign for a second.

New ministers are not immune from this kind of harassment. They are, in fact, prime targets for it, a big red bull's-eye having been painted on their foreheads at the climax of their installation services.

Once this basic scenario is laid out in a Pastoral Administration 101 bull session, the scary anecdotes from interns fresh out of the field-placement battlefield start piling up. These involve ☐ Mrs. Clawson, the tone-deaf, seventy-two-year-old Organist For Life at Third Presbyterian, locking the keyboard to the battered Hammond (she has the only key) in the middle of morning worship and stalking out of the church because little Sally Travleck chose to lisp a morning solo to the accompaniment of an Amy Grant backup tape. Results: three weeks of a cappella hymn singing, and the Travlecks move on to Brimstone Baptist.

☐ Mr. Broomfield, octogenarian vestryman, demanding an audit of the church's books for the past five years upon discovering that Cousin Millie's Memorial Fund was tapped for an earthquake relief offering instead of for the parlor-redecoration scheme Millie had requested with her last dying breath. Results: an unbudgeted $1,200 CPA bill, gridlock at the next three church council meetings while a new bequest policy is hammered out, and such a loss of face for the Very Reverend Dr. Hammerjammer that the man can't find his nose to blow it. And pink taffeta curtains in the parlor—out of operating funds.

☐ The Olsons' nonnegotiable suggestion that Reverend Accolia stop preparing her sermons from this newfangled lectionary thing and present an edifying topical series on "Dress Codes for Disciples," complete with sartorial criteria that Reverend Accolia herself couldn't meet with a $2,000 wardrobe budget and an updated Spiegel catalog. Result: the third convention of a search committee in five years—Mrs. Olson, chairperson.

Such, we clerical boot-campers come to imagine, are the vicissitudes of life in the typical mainline-to-moderate congregation—median age threescore-and-something, sludged in and suffocating from years of rigid domination by members who want their grandchildren baptized, Sunday-schooled, confirmed and turned out just as they themselves were fifty years previously by old, authoritarian Pastor Pete, the last minister who had any notion of how to whip these recalcitrant believers into line. (Never mind that the grandchildren in question have long since moved to Bakersfield or Raleigh or Shrewsbury with their spiritually lapsed parents and only show up at the church to turn the VBS upside-down on their annual summer visit with Poppy and Nanna.)

Now, before I provoke a boycott by the American Association of Retired Persons with the foregoing, let me remind all of us that what I have presented thus far is a working hypothesis engendered by grapevine legend. True, this hypothesis packs enough of a wallop that for the first few months of my placement I tiptoed around the narthex of Zion Community Church as if treading on Christmas-tree bulbs, recoiling and ashen any time a gray-haired parishioner tapped me on the shoulder to ask if I would unlock the copier room.

The *reality* of the situation, however, is this: The seniors in the congregation I pastor form a phalanx of forty-three doting great-aunts and uncles who, in the past eight months, have prayed, hugged and backed me through whatever initial successes I have tallied, and who have protected me like a wall of cotton batting against the just results of some of my flakier initiatives.

It was Mr. Molecki who stood up at the Annual Budget Meeting and shamed his siblings in Christ into upping a salary package I was perfectly content with to include a medical allowance that covered the denominational health-care deductible. (How this man knew that our six-year-old, Alistair, would need four expensive strep tests before Easter, I can't say.)

It was Mrs. Pope who eased my entry into the Dorcas Circle prayer group by gushing weekly about how fine it was that I took time from my busy schedule to meet with them. (I had previously blocked out 9:00-10:00 a.m. Wednesdays in my Daytimer for straightening paper clips and was relieved to have an Official Midweek Duty.)

And it was Mrs. Markham who comforted me through her husband's funeral, the first at which I had presided, and which was made all the more agonizing by the fact that Mr. Markham had taken an intentional overdose of pain pills in the face of inoperable cancer. ("Roy was so proud of being on the search committee that found you, and he would have been prouder if he could have seen the way you handled his memorial service." I'd managed not to cry until she said that.)

Oh, Violet Mason crabbed a bit about my mustache, and there was a rumbling or two over the time it had taken me to visit certain homes, but by Pentecost, I was essentially aghast at the slanders I had been prepped with in regard to Senior Saints.

Actually, I think the patriarchs and matriarchs of the local church are misunderstood for understandable reasons. The trepidation they inspire in fledgling clergypeople is based on a **true** enough premise. Many elder statesmen and women have **indeed** made a second—or even a first—home in their Christian **family**, and their investment in its well-being (yes, and even in some of its more arcane traditions) is tenacious.

The faulty reasoning that follows from this premise, however, is that the Old Guard are obstructionists, when in fact their devotion to the structures they have labored so faithfully and sacrificed so unremittingly to build, and looked to their Lord so hopefully to preserve, ranks them among the most forward-looking members in the body.

I suppose they can be and often are—much to the irritation of some bright, hard-charging soul who has just been cranked out of the denominational machinery—resistant to needed change. But the simple truth is that they ache to have what they constructed under the Holy Spirit's supervision survive them.

They want the rug rats who crash into them in the foyer to meet Jesus Christ in the same church-camp pine copse where they met him. They want the young couples embarked on the white-capped ocean of marriage to have the same anchor they had. They want the halting, powerful testimonies to God's ability to rearrange the pieces of a scattered life to echo through the sanctuary long after their own witness has been silenced.

And if that wanting is sometimes expressed in bewilderment or anxiety or even low-wattage carping, what's the harm in listening a little longer and a little harder, or in allowing the Ugly-with-a-capital-U dried-flower arrangement that LaVara Harris made for some long-forgotten potluck to remain on the Communion table for a few more years?

Peace, Violet. The mustache stays, but so do a lot of other things.

4
Counseling Your Average Moral Hyena

Truth #4: People not only know they're sinful—they think they're *uniquely* awful.

The confession I'm about to make needs background so that it will be properly startling.

First of all, I'm a real hybrid where basic anthropology is concerned. My psyche is a repressed-fifties stock model—AA41, cold and distrustful with a chrome-plated emotional intake valve.

Nonetheless, my ideological wonder years coincided without remainder with the most florid segment of the sixties and seventies. Result: my understanding of human nature was grotesquely customized to accommodate an indelible optimism about the possibility of change and the power of good intentions, an optimism so boundless and buoyant it would make Phil Donahue gag, Leo Buscaglia blush and Jean-Jacques Rousseau himself commence cryptside 360s.

We're not finished. A religious conversion and theological reversal overlaid all of this. Observation and reflection led me to take the Fall seriously. Very seriously. I came to believe that Jonathan Edwards was soft on sin. I began to reject modern hymnody on the grounds that it uses the terms *wretch* and *worm* too infrequently. And you know, I still believe that it is impossible to underestimate the selfishness and viciousness lying below the psychic surface of—oh, everybody.

How this works out in practice is that I view anyone I meet as worthless swamp scum with inherent dignity and tremendous potential for growth.

Now look, aren't we all a little confused on this point? Willfully inconsistent? When "The Greatest Love of All" was an urban youth anthem and nothing more, I could get as teary as the next person listening to a class of graduating eighth-graders at an elementary school in the projects belt out the living truth that "learning to love yourself is . . ." etc., etc., etc.

And yet when the same tune, a few years later, reached heavy rotation on contemporary hits (read "Soft Rock for Young Moderns") playlists, the vision of a well-groomed MBA sitting at a downtown stoplight with the sunroof of his BMW open and his Blaupunkt going full blast as he yowled out the very same lyrics over Whitney Houston's vocals . . . well, let's just say that, at the time, a chunk of concrete through the windshield seemed like a measured response.

This whole conflict between more sanguine and more pessimistic assessments of, and prescriptions for, human nature was articulated better than I'm now doing in a well-known debate in the fifties between psychologist Carl Rogers and theologian Reinhold Niebuhr.

Rogers, famous for his client-centered therapy, argued that

people need affirmation, affirmation and more affirmation in order to thrive. Niebuhr, the champion of neo-Reformed Christian realism, countered with an incisive theological critique ("Phooey," or some such) and argued that the human soul was already so bloated with egocentrism that it was ready to burst like a ripe pimple.

In theory, as I studied the fine points of the matter in seminary, I sided with the Kraut. (Actually, Niebuhr was Krauto-American.) My plan, accordingly, as I stepped into the ministerial role, was to preach sin and judgment straight up to the twisted souls who had entrusted themselves to my pastoral care.

Now the confession: It's taken me six months with "the Rev" affixed to my name for me to flip-flop again. Reinhold and I were wrong. Rogers was right. Telling the average struggling parishioner that he or she is shamefully self-centered and sorrowfully tainted with greed, lust, pride and evil is like telling an Ethiopian famine victim that he or she needs to put a few pounds of meat on the old bones; it is a noxious statement of the screamingly obvious, and cruel to boot.

Let's face it: the run of apparently well-adjusted, self-actualized, functioning churchgoers—of whom the normal, healthy, unexceptional congregation at Zion Community Church is made up—reveal themselves, once the door to the pastor's office is closed behind them, to be one sad litter of whipped puppies. People, in the most generic sense, *just don't like themselves.* What's more, the auto-reproach mechanisms in most heads and hearts have long since gone into overdrive for what seem to the observer to be pitifully inadequate reasons. It's one thing to feel properly remorseful for a life of Hitlerian viciousness or Jaggeresque debauchery. But how many times in my short reign as Father Confessor have I observed sweet, decent people struggle for weeks with their own shamed reticence, until one day they finally offer up the tearful admission that they once called God a "doodyhead" or that they had actual sex with a high-school sweetheart?

Reading over the last paragraph, I realize what so astounds me about most persons' nonexistent self-esteem. Most of us not only think we're awful—we think we're uniquely awful. Try the following exercise: In the next seven days, pay attention to the number of times the word *crazy* shows up in the following context: "I know this sounds crazy, but . . ." or "You're going to think I'm crazy when I tell you that . . ."

In counseling sessions I started out dismissing "Isn't that crazy?" as a verbal mannerism (akin to "Y'know?"), until I began to realize that *people mean it*. They really do think that they're alone and abnormal in hating parents who beat the hell out of them. They really do think they're bad and bizarre for loving someone who doesn't love them back. They really do consider themselves not just shameful but *weird* shameful for wishing from time to time that the twins had never been born . . . for taking secret delight in smug Cousin Susie's divorce . . . for giving Ed over in the Parts Department a bigger-than-allowable employee discount on the sofa set. Quasi-pathetic, no?

You were right all along, Carl, and it takes a man as big as I to admit it. I'll even admit it gladly, because there's a payoff for recognizing that I have been misdiagnosing the human heart all these years. My new insight, you see, has allowed me to develop a stunningly simple yet remarkably effective counseling technique. As long as I'm not dealing with a parishioner who's deeply neurotic or who's struggling with 40-weight emotional sludge from the past, I've come to realize that I can get ace results from the following therapeutic intervention.

| PERSON IN MY OFFICE: | I know this is going to sound crazy, but [gives example of something he or she thinks makes him or her sound like a moral hyena and a loon to boot, but which is, in reality, perfectly understandable and, to a merciful and patient God, no big stretch, if any, to forgive]. |
| ME: | [with unfeigned sincerity] Nope. That doesn't sound crazy at all. [Visibly thinking it over to make sure I'm not mistaken.] Huh-uh. It's just not crazy. I, for the life of me, can't see the craziness in it. Just a real normal reaction there. |

I swear on the Bible (New International Version with Study Notes and Maps of the Holy Land) that people brighten noticeably when I so vouch for their sanity and their humanity.

I challenge you to try this at home. The next time someone unburdens their soul to you and waits for you to confirm their awfulness, dispense a little grace instead, in Christ's name. You're going to think I'm crazy, but I tell you—it works.

5
Never Trust a Spiritual Revolution You Can't Dance To

Truth #5: The real problem with the New Age movement is that it tries to make us think we can control our fate.

I went to the hospital to see my friend Bob last week. The bedside conversation centered on Bob's wife, Helen, on his children and grandson, on what I was up to at the church, and on my hopes for the restoration of Bob's health.

It was an innocuous enough chat, but also a sad one, because I was doing all the talking. Bob was lying in a coma and couldn't answer back. He had been operated on the month before for a brain aneurysm, and had never woken up. Still hasn't. And now he's contending with pneumonia and meningitis as well.

The aneurysm is just another in a long series of bad breaks Bob has endured. A hard and honest worker all his life, skilled in refrigeration and a host of other repair and maintenance functions, Bob has endured career disappointments and a long struggle to make ends meet. He has battled depression. He was wiped out in a flood a few years back. Finally, he had found a reasonably peaceful retirement, squeezing by on social security and a part-time job, living close to a doting grandchild, doing handyman work for family and friends, settling into a contented enough routine—and then a blood vessel in his head went and betrayed him, ballooning out and leaking blood into his skull.

A common enough tragedy, I suppose, but the heck of it is, Bob is a truly nice man. *Nice,* of course, is an adjective generally thought of as noncommittal. To call someone "nice" is customarily to damn him or her with faint praise. But by calling Bob "nice," I mean to award a rare accolade.

Last winter my car broke down near Bob and Helen's house. They put me up for the night and fed me, and in the morning Bob endured the remnants of a blustery snowstorm to jerry-rig my carburetor so I could pick up my wife and sons at the airport. Nothing extraordinary, just common decency, common hospitality.

Bob has never been a drinker, never run around on his wife, never been harsh with his family. He has loved justice, practiced mercy and walked humbly with his God. Simple enough virtues, these are, until you stop and think about how few people that you know practice them. Bob is just a good man, and a fat lot of good it's done him.

OK. I'm about ready to mount the soapbox again, and this time the New Age is my target. So what has all this got to do with New Age religion? Something, I think.

"Wait now," you're probably interjecting at this point. "Is he trying to forge a facile link between the satanic seduction of contemporary spiritual syncretism and the pull-yourself-up-by-your-own-Reebok-laces, name-it-and-claim-it brand of Yankee exuberance that we've all come to know and love?"

Well, yes, I suppose I am. What of it? Look at the consensus that homelessness and hunger are avoidable realities endured by shiftless no-goods. Look at the current fashionable-if-subdued antagonism toward nonwhites in the U.S. ("Here we've long since eradicated all the barriers that used to hold them back, and they *still* go around screaming about racism and 'rights.' Do these people know no gratitude?") Look even at the relatively benign "just do it" school of physical fascism, which proclaims that anyone willing to put in the sweat can and should nurture the cardiovascular network of a Carl Lewis and the Adonis-like pectorals of an Arnold Schwarzenegger (or at least a Cher).

Is it really that big a stretch from these phenomena to the confident assertion that only sniveling sloth, willful ignorance and spiritual cowardice prevent us from ascending into the ontological Hall of Fame? Is New Age thought really any more, at base, than blaming the victim on a cosmic scale?

Lest we get sidetracked here by red herrings, let me say that I'm all for personal accountability—to a point. Even my friend Bob made choices—jobs that he took or didn't take, forty years of smoking which had significant bearing on the course of his life and health. But the realities of our complicity in our own misfortune need to be put in a larger perspective that New Age religion fails to satisfactorily provide.

In combating the teachings of Pelagius (I've got to make some use of those divinity-school courses on church history— you remember, the British monk who promoted Taking Control of Your Own Eternal Destiny long before most of Shirley Mac-Laine's soul's host bodies were anything more than twinkles in their respective fathers' eyes?), St. Augustine hammered away repeatedly at a theme to which he was driven as much by acute empirical observation as by biblical understanding and dogmatic conviction: Something about the human race and the world it inhabits continually frustrates the human ambition to live well and happily.

You see, in the prevalent hoo-hah over the Coming Reign of Spiritual Enlightenment, there's been one common thread that has really disturbed me. It's not the crystals or the flying saucers, not the goofy theories about reincarnation and channeling or the "I Survived the Atlantis Meltdown" bumper stickers, not even the heterodox speculations of ditzy celebrities or the fire-walking freak shows. (OK, the Windham Hill records *have* bugged me pretty much. Never trust a spiritual revolution you can't dance to.)

No, what strikes me as the true ideological bummer of the Aquarian onslaught is the underlying New Age tenet that we are in complete control of our fate, and that the sadness which is an inextricable component of the human tragicomedy is, in reality, something we either overcome by our own rigorous effort or bear as the justified punishment for our inability to overcome. New Age thought, in virtually all of its manifestations, dictates that we are the captains—or General Al Haigs— of our own fate: "No problem. I'm in charge here."

Rigorously applied, this theory makes a mockery of the lousiness of every lousy thing that happens. Is my friend Bob lying unconscious in an ICU bed? Tough darts. He's responsible for his own aneurysm. Are other friends struggling to shake off the effects of a childhood with an alcoholic parent? Enough whining. They're willing accomplices to their own misery. Are Sudanese children lying in a ditch, dazed by starvation and shell-shocked from the booming tanks that regularly rumble through their villages? Hey—it's not a pretty lifestyle, but *they picked it.*

The denizens of Harmonic Convergence Land, when you pry off all the sensationalistic parapsychic adornments with which they bedeck themselves, are little more than the latest avatars (pardon the Easternism) of the tantalizing yet ultimately callous perfectionism that has always beguiled the human mind. By underestimating and oversimplifying evil, such perfectionism (the Christian incarnations of which could fill a history book) perennially promises freedom. What it almost always delivers instead (read 1 Corinthians carefully) is social and spiritual elitism. It cruelly condemns the already burdened and salves all the wrong consciences.

That its visibility is increasing now is lamentable, but makes perfect sense when you consider that its outlook accords nicely with the present American Zeitgeist.

Augustine's insistence on the thoroughness with which sin permeates our existence (though it may, as academic sharpie Elaine Pagels argues in her book *Adam, Eve and the Serpent,* have been pushed to overstatement) recapitulates understandings taken up by great minds that preceded his, and has itself been recapitulated by great minds that have drawn from him. But let's not take the word of Jeremiah and Paul and Calvin and Luther and Reinhold Niebuhr and Flannery O'Connor on this. Let's just note that the doctrine of original sin—the teaching that not only do we fail to do the good we would do and do the evil that we would avoid, but unavoidable evil seems, for the present, to be built into the system—seems to fit the data into which most of us slam on a daily basis.

In our encounters with our own and others' missteps and misfortunes, it is in the millennia-old Christian struggle with the complex roots of suffering, and not in the glib prescriptions of supposedly modern supposed enlightenment, that we find the wellspring of humane insight. The Old and New Testaments and the classic formulations that emerged from them plausibly explain the human predicament—even while sternly refusing to excuse our participation in it, and gently urging us beyond it.

New Age nostrums would convince me simply that Bob is his own worst enemy. I am more convinced that Bob has fallen prey in his life to many enemies—genetic and environmental imperfections, laws of physics and probability, powers and principalities, self and others—all of which have, in the present confluence of their effects, "conspired and lurked and watched his steps, eager to take his life," and with which he now has to reckon. If the ambiguity of this conviction leaves me more puzzled, angry and unconsoled than would neater solutions to the riddle of Bob's dilemma, then so be it.

In the meantime, I am further convinced that Bob has, in addition to his enemies, a Friend whose concern is finally more determinative of the outcome of his existence than is the malignity of the foes that have dogged him. In this matter too, I find New Age religion woefully inadequate to represent reality.

6
The Prophet Edgar
(and Other Unlikely Heroes)

Truth #6: Terms defined in seminary take
on new meaning in the local church.

Definitions. Seminary was chock-full of definitions.
The nature of God was defined. The true essence of
the church was defined. Our chance of avoiding
youth work in our first assignment after ordination was defined.
(Coupled in a ratio with 1, it involved the inverse of an expo-
nential number.)

Definitions are necessary. They are comforting. Also, insofar
as they lead to expectations about what ministry will be like
once one leaves the theory-encrusted walls of divinity school,
they are grossly inadequate.

What follows are three definitions of terms that are freely
bandied about in the parlance of church professionals. These
definitions take the form of vignettes and portraits that illus-
trate the concepts of testimony, prophecy and witness. They are

suggestive rather than didactic. Where they appear to conflict
with set assumptions, consider them supplementary to rather
than antithetical to those assumptions. But consider them.

Testimony
Esther was a girl—a young woman who lived at the group home
in the neighborhood and started coming to church with her
friend/enemy/friend Marie.

Marie was more or less well-behaved. She would sit in the
front row past the angled pews and smile her beatific smile
throughout the whole service.

When we said the Lord's Prayer, she would always be a sentence behind—"the kingdom and the power and the glory," she
said when the rest of us were saying "Amen" and looking for
the ushers to come down the aisle for the offering. She would
sing loud and off-key and a line behind, and then she would sit
down and smile her smile, and we all liked her. She fit the
blueprint for one of the Little Ones Jesus talked about—those
we should care for and avoid giving scandal to.

Esther was not well-behaved. She talked loudly during the
sermon and occasionally bickered with Marie. Once she
brought a retarded young man who she said was her boyfriend,
and they made out—there's no other way of putting it—
throughout the service. After that, he never came back with her.

During the announcements, when the business of the church
and prayer concerns were shared from the front, Esther loved
to come forward and speak. She would tell us to pray for her
father in South Carolina who was very sick and about to die.
The next week she would beg our prayers for her sister, who had
broken her back and was expected to be paralyzed. Two weeks
later, she'd implore prayer again for the soul of her father, who

had died, and a month or two later she would ask us to pray for her father and her aunt and her sister, who lived in Utah and had no money because her father was out of a job.

Once she came forward and said that she loved God because he was Jesus, and she wanted to sing a song to him that she had just learned. Before anyone could object, she grabbed the microphone from its stand as though she were a pro, stepped out in front of the Communion table, bowed her head for a second and then began to *screech* a song of praise that she made up as she went along.

"Ohhhhhh . . . FATHER in HEAVEN," she howled, "I loooooooooooove youuuuuuu. / I love you Jesus. / You are GOOD to me. / I went to Kansas last week. / I looooooove you God. / Thank you for Jesus. / Ohhhhh . . . heavenly Father."

It sounded like barn owls in a flurry. She sang in no identifiable key. The song was interminable, and we all looked at one another, wondering who would go grab the mike from her and thank her for sharing and lead her back to her seat, but no one did.

After two minutes of singing (do you *know* how long two minutes is?), she redeposited the microphone on its stand and returned to her seat. We never saw her in church again after that Sunday.

Prophecy

No one can recall when Edgar was appointed to the church board. My guess is that he received his call to serve as membership elder during a gas leak at the local chemical plant, when a long-forgotten nominating committee was overcome by noxious psychotropic fumes and was not legally responsible for its judgments.

Because of a long-standing tradition at Zion Community
Church that once a brother or sister in Christ has made it onto
the board he or she is not removed until death or relocation (or,
as happens with elders who possess an ounce of lucidity or
theological reflectiveness or administrative acumen, until he or
she begs off after a couple of years due to career or family
pressure), Edgar had served in the ecclesiastical power structure
for seventeen years.

Edgar could be counted on to lengthen any meeting in which
he participated by a solid forty-five minutes. In his quest to
make sure that no decision arrived at in the councils of the
church ignored even the most niggling option or implication, he
dragged out the discussion of every item of business intermi-
nably. His questions and objections in these parlays were always
illogical or trivial or tangential or, in some instances, all three.
(On these occasions, word would buzz around Zion for weeks
that Edgar had "pulled a triple" at a recent meeting.)

Edgar was a late incarnation of Emily LaTella, the old Gilda
Radner character, only with less charm. And he *never* said
"Never mind."

One Monday evening after long hours of wading through
routine business, the church board came to an offhand request
by a local battered-women's shelter. The shelter, Rachel's
House, was being pressured by its neighbors to relocate because
of the "unhealthy climate" it created in the community. Rachel's
House had the funds to build a new shelter and needed an
expanded capacity anyway. What its directors were looking for
was a site. One of its board members heard from one of our
board members that Zion Community Church owned several
parcels of land in the neighborhood of the church building.
Feelers had gone out. Would we be willing to add the lot we

owned on the block in back of us to their list of options? Thanks to a recent grant, they could afford to make an attractive offer for it.

No harm in toying with the idea, our treasurer opined, even if there would be a lot of paperwork involved. No harm, a second voice chimed in, except that a few years ago we raised the possibility of putting a play lot on the land. No harm at all, another elder offered, except that land values around here are rising and if we want to do a building addition in a few years we'll be glad we hung onto the property so that we can get more money for it and make a good down payment on a new fellowship hall.

Eventually, the "no harm" preamble to the lukewarm statements being offered was dropped. "We have to think about *our* neighbors," the outreach elder cautioned. "If they don't care for a shelter in their community, cooperation in acquiring one could be devastating to our witness."

The recording clerk, who lived two doors down from the church, affirmed that the people who lived in the immediate community had as much right to consideration as potential clients of Rachel's House, besides which, shelter personnel were known to encourage women to leave their husbands, and that did not accord with biblical teaching on the sanctity of marriage.

The comment irked the moderator, who had been a Rachel's House board member in the mid-seventies and who, in a sharp tone of voice, characterized the potential land sale as a "win-win" situation for the parties involved. A board member who was a lawyer opined that it might turn into a "lose-lose" situation if the church could be held liable down the road for disruptions of the peace traceable to the shelter's relocation.

The debate continued for almost an hour, during which time Edgar was strangely (for him) silent. Fears about long-term repercussions over the land sale were pitted against potential monetary benefits. Tempers frayed. Opinions were expressed, modified, changed altogether.

Caution began to carry the day. Zoning hassles and the prospect of lucrative benefits from a delay of the land sale swayed consensus toward a polite, even regretful refusal to add our lot to the site list. Just as we were about to nix the whole idea and move on, Edgar spoke up.

"My daughter," he said, "got beat up awful bad by the first fellow she was married to out in New Jersey, and no one helped her—not her church, not the police, no one. Here we are talking about whether or not to sell our land to these people, and all we can think about is who we might make mad and how much we might get somewhere down the line, like money and our reputation are all that matter. Why are we arguing about whether or not we should sell our lot to these people instead of whether we should charge 'em a little bit of money for it or just give it to 'em outright?"

The meeting was over six minutes later. Zion Community Church's offer to deed the lot behind it over to Rachel's House was declined that winter due to the availability of a more central location and a matching grant from the federal government that had to be used toward land acquisition.

Witness

Althea crocheted yellow elephants.

It doesn't show up on the apostle Paul's list of gifts in 1 Corinthians 12, but that's what she did. Plush cushions of golden yarn bundled into a rotund body, a mesh net pulled over a Styrofoam ball for the head, a few strands of braided string for a tail, stout purled legs, and white points of sewn felt protruding from either side of the stout knit trunk, with button eyes and a satin half-moon mouth.

Althea invariably included a little calligraphy note with her zoological creations, tucked into the spaces on the animal's torso. "From 'tusk'-to-dawn, Jesus loves you. Zion Community Church," the script read.

Church members speculated whether the Zion Community name could be copyrighted so that we could legally proscribe its inclusion on the sides of fabric elephants. It's not that anyone begrudged Althea her hobby. It's just that the distribution of her handicraft projects was so ubiquitous.

Here we were, adopting a sophisticated, denominationally sponsored program of personal witness, sharing a carefully contextualized gospel to select demographic groups out of a consideration for their felt needs and articulated aspirations, reaching out to unchurched community members with a measured approximation of the scriptural message of God's concern. And there was Althea, mass-producing her yarn elephants and forcing them on every Vacation Bible School attendee and visiting congregant and guest speaker who came along.

She bragged one winter Sunday that after the pipes in the trailer house she occupied had frozen and a workman from a local plumbing firm had dropped by to unclog them, she had sent him home with a handwritten promissory note for services rendered and a Jesus elephant for his eighteen-month-old daughter. (Since the elephant tied her to us, we seriously considered paying the bill out of church funds so that "Zion Community Church" would not become synonymous with "Chiselers for Christ.")

The week after Althea died of complications from pneumonia, there was an article on the Saturday religion page of the
local newspaper about "The Passing of the Elephant Lady." The
column, with two pictures (one of Althea at a senior citizens'
luncheon, the other a closeup of one of her elephants), detailed
our late member's penchant for fabric arts and estimated that
before her passing she had manufactured over eight hundred
crocheted pachyderms. The news piece was pure small-town
froth, and it included the information that Althea had been
supported in her hobby by her friends at the Zion Church.

The next day there was a new family in the Zion pews. It was
headed by a thirty-six-year-old single mom who had drifted
away from church after a Methodist upbringing, but who had
wanted her kids raised under a Christian influence. She had
read about Althea the day before, and she figured that any
group of people who had encouraged an old woman to do a
lovely thing like give out stuffed animals to local children was
worth checking out.

Her twelve-year-old son started attending Sunday school the
next week and youth group the following month, and was baptized at the end of the summer.

7
A Worthy Adversary Relinquishes His Chainsaw

Truth #7: Chaperoning youth retreats is never as bad as people say—it's worse.

W e're having a youth retreat next month," senior-high leader Amy Molina informed me one Sunday morning. "Would you come along with us?"

A youth retreat? Would I come along? Heh, heh. Heh, heh, heh, heh. Breaking in the new pastor, are we, Amy? A youth retreat, huh . . . ?

Like many a late-model minister, I came to my position fresh from a long sentence in youth work—in my case, three-to-five with a parachurch teen group, plus two years of probation in a seminary field placement.

I cut my professional-church-leadership teeth on Thursday-night meetings with roomfuls of high-octane adolescents, roller-skating marathons at which I wielded a crowbar for separating overamorous couples in the dark corner beside the snack bar, three-Kleenex-box counseling sessions behind closed office doors with an enraged fifteen-year-old girl whose parents were so monstrous they wouldn't let her stencil "Motley Crue Rules" across her chest in indelible ink, the works.

In the six years before my ordination and escalation to full-service ministry, I ate more lukewarm pizza, led more barely postpubescent bull sessions on the ethics of tongue-kissing before marriage, refereed more church-league basketball games, played guitar for more Teen Sunday *Godspell* medleys, did more contact work in high-school cafeterias (more lukewarm pizza), jerry-rigged more broken-down van carburetors in the 5-degree parking lots of toboggan-run sites, and led more devotional prayers with one eye open so I could actually catch Jack Davis slugging his younger brother as we implored the Lord to intervene on behalf of world peace than any marginally sane human being should ever have to do.

And you, Amy Molina, with your Shedd's-Spread-wouldn't-melt-in-your-mouth smile, are asking me to come along on a youth retreat, thinking, no doubt, that in the process you will present me with a baptism by fire into the world of the pregrown-ups under my pastoral care?

I could tell you a thing or two about the sleepless, soda-spattered, nerve-uprooting approximation of the grimmest reaches of the underworld that is a Teen Overnight.

February 9-10, 1983, Amy. The dates are indelibly etched on my frontal lobes. Eighteen urban legal-age wannabes shipped out to a suburban conference camp with me and a female chaperon who promptly goes the migraine route fifteen minutes after arrival and gets sequestered in an unlit private suite, leaving *me,* Amy Molina, me alone and friendless to execute the weekend plan.

I struggle solo through Friday evening, with the help of a plate of raw meat (pieces of which I occasionally toss into the retreat-hall game room into which I've corralled my charges) and a 25-horsepower John Deere chainsaw that I have carefully tucked away (so I let the rumor spread) in my duffle bag underneath a stack of Reach Out New Testaments.

At bedtime—which has somehow drifted to the nether side of midnight despite a carefully scripted schedule—I herd the girls into their room and plant myself and my blankets at the doorway to the sleeping quarters that have been assigned to the boys.

All quiet for one night, yes? Amy, Amy, Amy, you naive young thing. Giggling and shuffling around in the dark—punctuated by my increasingly irritated calls for quiet—occupy the next half-hour, the first stage of Teen Maneuvers. Dirty jokes just below the level of chaperon audibility usher in the next phase. More calls for sleep and silence. Can you say "All right you guys, now quiet down and *this time I really mean it"* many, many times in a row?

Cut to the chase. By 3:00 a.m. I am engaged in something more than chaperoning and something less than a full-scale police action in the midst of a Caribbean coup attempt, but only slightly less. Pillows and hamburger buns are flying through the air, two kids in the corner are having an aerosol deodorant fight, and one boy has sneaked through my entrenched position and is hovering over a sleeping girl in the next room with pencils taped to his fingers, playing Freddy Krueger in hopes of inducing an amusing case of cardiac defibrillation.

By 3:10, Amy Molina, I . . . have lost it. The last thing I remember is roaring in rage like a bull stuck by a picador, grasping sleeping bags by the bottom and dumping out the occupants (who have suddenly decided that feigning sleep is the

better part of valor), grabbing my charges by the arm and fling-
ing them into their new bunking assignments, which are wher-
ever they land along the edge of the wall. (Note, Amy, that in
less than five hours I am supposed to be leading a postbreakfast
Bible study on the fruits of the Spirit—peace, patience, kind-
ness, etc., etc.)

By 3:30 a.m. quiet reigns, and I have this little vein on the
lower reaches of my temple throbbing uncontrollably.

The next morning brings mumbled apologies and an awk-
ward start to the program day. I have survived, but my re-
sources are spent. I realize that I will never make it to our
scheduled Sunday-evening departure without either an extended
Saturday-afternoon Happy Hour or . . . a plan. Yes, that's it. I'll
need a plan.

That, Amy Molina, is when inspiration strikes. I line up a
VCR from the conference camp coordinator and pay a visit to
the nearest video-rental store. We romp through the day's
planned program, an endless parade of Teen Talks, Nerf hockey
games, snack breaks and nature walks, and then, when the
Witching Hour strikes (9:00 p.m., Amy, when adolescent hor-
mones start slamming around in the confined space of a hyper-
active teenage body), I gather my charges in the Rec Hall and
punch in the Beta version of *Psycho*. I let that run its course
and then program the second feature—the old Audrey Hepburn
chestnut *Wait Until Dark*.

By midnight the youth group has absorbed three hours of
psychopathic mayhem and blood-soaked object lessons on the
foolishness of roaming solo in dimly lit corridors. By 12:15 a.m.
the kids are huddled together in their sleeping bags in wide-eyed
terror. No, I don't get to sleep until 1:00 a.m., but it's not
because I'm breaking up brawls. It's because three kids have full

bladders and none of them wants to chance the washroom un-escorted. One of the girls—I'm not sure she's showered after dusk to this day.

I won, Amy. I faced down the Beast that is a group of high-school students on retreat, *and I won.*

And now you want me to escort our kids to Camp Kilian in hopes of *initiating* me?

Bring 'em on.

* * *

Oh.

Assignment completed. I'm back from Camp Kilian. It was, uh, fine. It went fine.

No, it didn't either. I'm still trying to get my bearings. It started off well enough. An hour out of town we pulled into a minimart, Amy and Sid Molina in the church van with most of the kids and the luggage, me in my Subaru wagon with two of the tenth-grade guys. Amy was chewing out a couple of the teens from her vehicle for having a popcorn fight on the inter-state, and I, bored from listening in my car to an extended conversation about Mrs. Travis's history class, volunteered to drive along with Sid and keep things calm. (I should've sensed something was up when Freddy Logan started to call Mrs. Tra-vis a bad name and then blushed and changed the subject when he noticed I was monitoring the discussion.)

When I climbed into the passenger seat of the van, the energy level within diminished noticeably.

"You riding in here, Pastor?"

"Yup. Watch out now."

Three of the girls in the third seat pulled out pillows from behind their duffle bags and promptly curled up for a nap that lasted for the duration of the trip. Sid and I talked college football until we arrived.

What happened then? Well, not nothing, but as much of an approximation of it as I've ever witnessed in a cluster of human beings with a median age under eighteen.

We talked a bunch, ate some (these kids had the real annoying habit of asking if they could take my plate back to the cleanup window for me), talked some more, indulged in a half-hearted game of Capture the Flag in the evening . . . oh yeah, the Capture the Flag game. It was a disaster. No one got hurt, no one sneaked off to the periphery of the camp to down a smuggled six-pack of malt liquor, and when, after a stealthy half-hour of crawling through dead leaves on my belly, I grabbed the opposing team's flag and started to make a run for it, the guys guarding the enemy's base just kind of stood there and stared at me sheepishly as I lit out for my own territory.

"Why didn't you take me prisoner?" I asked, huffing and puffing, as we all trudged back to the main building.

"Uh, I don't know," Freddy shrugged, and he and Cody Weisner exchanged glances and giggled.

"What? What?" I asked.

"Well," Cody offered offhandedly, "geez, Pastor, we didn't want you to go be having a coronary with us running after you. We were watching you crawl in and, you know, you were turning real red in the face. You're our new minister and my parents would be real pis—um, mad if we killed you off."

So we went inside and had hot chocolate, and then I gathered the kids in the meeting room, assembled them in front of a video unit and announced that we were all going to watch a real scary movie before bed.

"What movie, Pastor?" Sarah Molina asked, snapping her gum.

"It's called *Psycho*."

You could hear eyes rolling in their sockets.

"We've seen that, Pastor. It's dead. It's not even in color. *Psycho III* was better. You should see the blood spurt when they cut that guy's head off."

"You know what was really excellent?" asked Cody of his peer group. *"Friday the 13th Part VI."*

"Oh, yeahhh," the others chorused.

"You really saw guts come out in that," one kid reflected admiringly.

"I'm tired," Sarah said. "I'm going to bed. The rest of you guys coming?"

And off they trooped, the young women to their quarters, the young men to theirs. "Good night, Mr. and Mrs. Molina," they sang out as they exited. "Good night, Pastor."

"I have a *name,* you know," I shouted after them.

Sid and I played gin for half an hour, and then we went to bed too. To sleep. It was 10:45.

Driving home the following evening, Sid told me about last year's retreat, undertaken without the presence of my predecessor. "It was a nightmare," he recollected. "No sleep, kids disappearing, schedule way off track. Good thing you came along this time. I won't even have to take a day off work to recuperate."

So that was it. My suspicions were confirmed. It was me. The killjoy with the collar had ensured a tranquil weekend. That's why Amy had requested the honor of my presence. The roughhousing, the rowdiness, the disrespect that I had worked years to earn had been killed off by my ordination. In one year, by virtue of a simple laying on of hands, I had gone from a Worthy Adversary to (can my trembling fingers even type out the words?) an Authority Figure.

I'm seriously disillusioned. I wanted to become a minister. Somehow I wound up a Grownup in the bargain. Amy Molina, what have you done to me?

8
Paul Plants, Apollos Waters, Karl Frets

Truth #8: You can't measure success in the church, but maybe it doesn't hurt to try.

In my inaugural sermon at Zion Community Church, I preached from 1 Corinthians 3:6: "I planted the seed, Apollos watered it, but God made it grow."

I reminded the congregation that in the partnership in ministry that lay ahead of us, we would plan many worship services, implement many programs, support many missions both locally and internationally, and together proclaim and seek to embody the gospel of Jesus Christ. All of our busyness together, however (I solemnly warned), would come to naught if we failed to recognize and perpetually reaffirm that we are only agents about our Father's business, and that only as we become channels for the Holy Spirit's power working within us would we bear true fruit for the kingdom of God.

It was a great sermon. I was eloquent. I was passionate. I was visionary. I was scriptural.

I was also, as it turns out, bluffing.

Lest I be accused of bad faith (in both senses of the term), though, let me affirm that I believed what I was saying—at the time.

I came up through the ecclesiastical ranks in an era of Young Turk deprofessionalization. The prevailing currents of my spiritual and vocational formative years flowed toward mutuality, empowerment of the "laity" (that last a suspect term anyway, a vestige of clergy-congregation polarization) and the rejection of worldly models of achievement in favor of allowing the winds of the Spirit to blow whither they would, never minding concrete results. (Does "we're not called to be successful—we're called to be *faithful*" ring any bells?)

We up-and-comers chuckled knowingly as our pastoral mentors—middle-aged converts from the Do-It-Yourself Achievement Syndrome—ruefully described for us their years wandering in the wilderness of career advancement based on the Great Mores: more members on the church rolls, more money in the church coffers, more square footage in the church plant.

Our mirth—the good humor of cocksure Timothys listening to these repentant Pauls—was mixed with condescending pity. How could our elders have become so trapped in the scramble for scalps, shekels and sanctuaries? How could they have fallen so easily into the Babylonian lock-step that had led them out of the promised land of simple spiritual self-forgetting? How could they have been dazzled so by grubby *doing* that they lost sight of the virtues of holy *being?*

Great questions. Here are some more, arising from a tenure of less than a year in my own pastorate: Can we just, like, forget that I was ever that smug? Could someone recall for me exactly when I myself wandered across the Babylon city limits? And, uh, oh let's see, one more query for stylistic balance—OK, how about "Where did you say they put the exit ramp back onto the straight and narrow path of pastoral purity?"

See, as long as I feel that I'm practicing my vocation with integrity, I truly don't care if the membership ranks swell or not. So why have I lost consecutive nights of increasingly precious sleep because the Bucholzes haven't come back into the fold after checking out my first few sermons, and because the Jorgensens ended up joining Good Shepherd Lutheran in spite of the charming Sunday brunch we threw them?

And really, I don't concern myself with the mundane mechanics of annual budgets and such. So why has the drop in per-member giving for the third quarter left me unaccountably depressed, while I face with tranquil equanimity the teacher's verdict that my son needs to repeat kindergarten?

Well, at least I don't fret over irrelevant babbling from myopic parishioners about the pressing need for a capital construction program. So what explains the twenty sweaty hours I poured last week into modifying blueprints for a long-delayed addition to the Sunday school while I paid only token attention to the needs of three elderly congregants who are languishing in the denominational nursing home?

It's not that I've abandoned my earlier ideals. It's just that I haven't lived up to them.

Why not? Hmmm. All right, first I'll take the lumps I have coming to me like a brave little soldier. Only then will I attempt to ennoble my failings with some tricky, self-serving rationalizations.

None of us escape our rearing. It's one thing to say that worldly yardsticks for accomplishment are not part of my spiritual makeup. It's another thing altogether to forgo making Mom and Dad (who've worked in business and the military) proud that I've prospered on their terms—kept the congregational balance sheets healthy, packed 'em in with my preaching, presided over the redecoration of the foyer with taste and elegance.

Yes, I have internalized the values of a previous generation more deeply than I'd care to admit. And no, that doesn't constitute a valid shift-of-blame for my uneasy preoccupation with numbers and accomplishments onto said generation. First off, I hate sniveling. ("Poor baby. He's been spoon-fed superficial criteria of self-worth until he's queasy and bloated . . . through no fault of his own." Nah. Not this little Rotarian.)

Second off, I'm the one who's transferred these values from spheres where they may be legitimate into a sphere where they aren't. Third off—irony ahead—Mom and Dad have long since signaled that *they* don't care much about "their terms" as applied to *my* current endeavors. They just want their bubby to be contented on whatever terms. (Don't you hate parents when they're sincerely noble?)

So back to the question at hand: Why isn't their little bubby contented, at least not with anything short of abundant tangible proof of his professional prowess? Why isn't he willing simply to plant and water and let God cause whatever growth, palpable or impalpable, is to be caused? Why is he acting so much like those sinecured, time-serving, career-minded clerics he professes to abhor?

Watch closely. Here's where I let myself off the hook.

I want to do this thing right. Really now. I want to be a good pastor. No, scalps, shekels and sanctuaries aren't the ultimate arbiters of whether I am a good pastor or not, but just what exactly is? We're into some wickedly fuzzy territory here. Measurements of any kind are hard to come by. Faithfulness is tough to quantify, except maybe in long-distance hindsight.

Be honest. Do you think Paul was altogether comforted, as he put his head on the Roman chopping block, that his recorded legacy was a handful of querulous house churches strung out along the backwaters of the Roman Empire? As Dorothy Day lay on her deathbed and reflected back upon decades of service to God, which was her more likely thought: "Lord, let thy servant now enter her rest" or "Geez, more derelicts downstairs. I'll bet no one's covering the night shift"? Don't you imagine that even the most outstanding of God's messengers wanted a little more hard evidence than they got that they weren't wasting their time or veering off course?

We're all happy enough to be storing our treasures in heaven where moths can't consume and rust can't destroy, but how do we even know whether we've got anything in our account up there? It's not like Pearly Gates Federal kicks out a statement every month. So in lieu of same, where's the feedback?

Forget the feedback, you say?

Live with the unknowing? Ride with the tension?

Right. Why don't I also turn in my Human Being union card right now and apotheosize ('Zat a word? Why not?) into a semidivine being who needs no evaluation or affirmation at all and is unconcerned whether in the main he is screwing up the people he works with or helping to improve their lives?

Sheesh.

All right, so the inaugural sermon at the next church gets amended. Paul plants, Apollos waters, Karl frets—about unspiritual barometers of what he can't help seeing as his own performance. Just like the calculating ministerial professional he swore he'd never be. Because maybe an unspiritual barometer beats having no such instrument at all. Because maybe letting your ego get all twisted up in your ministry in its own sick, warped, fallen way is not an unreasonable definition of giving a hoot.

Let those who have any problems with that cast the first adding machine.

9
Paint Boldly—
and Trust God

Truth #9: Don't try to evangelize with art;
don't try to make evangelism into great art.

You'll have to forgive me. I know I get to spout off at
least once a week, behind a pulpit. But some things
drive me to a soapbox any day of the week, not
just on Sundays. One of these things is what is euphemistically
called "Christian culture" (euphemistically "Christian" *and* euphemistically "culture").

I could begin here by asserting that, strictly, there is no such
thing as a "Christian" medium, that there are no "Christian"
cultural artifacts as such.

I could, if I chose, cite Luther on the Adiaphora, Kierkegaard
on the infinite qualitative distinction between things divine and
things human, Barth on the great gulf midst the utterly transcen-
dent Word of God and the purely limited words of God's creatures. (I do have a freshly minted seminary education, after all.)

I could, with justification, quote W. H. Auden, who said, "There can no more be a Christian art than there can be a Christian science or a Christian diet. There can only be a Christian spirit in which an artist, a scientist, works or does not work."

("I sometimes wonder," Auden goes on to write in his *Postscript: Christianity and Art,* "if there is not something a bit questionable, from a Christian point of view, about all works of art which make overt Christian references. They seem to assert that there is such a thing as a Christian culture, which there cannot be. Culture is one of Caesar's things.")

I could point out that, in its quest to extend its sectarian realm in all particulars, American evangelicalism has, ironically, fallen (à la Harvey Cox's goofy sixties classic *The Secular City)* into the classic liberal fallacy of baptizing into sanctity all sorts of merely temporal expressions and activities among its adherents.

I would be on defensible grounds in claiming that "Christian" music and radio, books and bookstores, films and videos, magazines, schools, barbershops, chiropractors, auto mechanics, home-sales schemes, lawyers and what-have-you are not only no more spiritually salutary than their "secular" counterparts, but actually less so in the sense that said counterparts at least don't aspire to unmerited identification with things holy.

I won't, however, do any of that.

Instead, I will accept the assumptions of common usage and take for granted that when we speak of "Christian" arts and entertainment and information, we are simply accepting certain conventions. In fact, we are discussing nothing more than the products of Christian believers who are trying to incorporate some of the perspectives granted them by their beliefs into work that seeks to educate or edify or amuse.

My motives for granting the possibility of "Christian" media, etc., are simple and pure. To put it plainly, how can you hope to ream something silly if you won't admit it exists?

That most of the byproducts of Christian publishing, recording, filmmaking and so on are richly reamable poses, of course, something of a dilemma. The recent case of Montana "hunters" who went after bison that strayed past the appointed limits of Yellowstone National Park comes to mind. It's hardly sporting, after all, to take potshots at a dumb beast that has lumbered so haplessly into one's sights; and yet it is undeniable also that, with its great girth and essential mindlessness, the silly animal fairly begs to be checked lest it infect and trample things of worth.

All right, then. Let's figure out what makes the conservative Protestant subculture the dreary mess that it is.

Can we agree, for starters, that much of what comes off the evangelical presses and out of the evangelical recording studios is simply of substandard quality—insipid, heavy-handed, poorly crafted?

Good—we're getting somewhere. Can we next reach consensus that much of what does pass technical muster (the writing is grammatical, the production values are adequate, an actual idea occasionally sneaks into play) is woefully derivative? Having said that Amy Grant does middle-of-the-road pop as well as Sheena Easton, or that Stryper does heavy metal as well as Quiet Riot, and granting that pop and heavy metal are defensible (if dispensable) genres if your tastes run that way, can we proceed to say that Amy Grant and Stryper don't do anything with pop or heavy metal that is creative or noteworthy?

I take for granted, of course, that slipping Jesus into some calcified format has nothing to do with "creative" or "noteworthy." The problem we're addressing, after all, is precisely that instead of following their own muses and developing forms and sensibilities that emerge naturally from their religious outlook, evangelical mediamongers seem always to glom onto some preestablished style or structure, and then to congratulate themselves for having produced "Christian" television newsmagazines or "Christian" hip-hop or "Christian" romance novels or "Christian" environmental symposia.

(I once received in the mail a "Christian" newspaper that attempted to knock off *USA Today* in every technical detail, right down to the *Weekly Reader* layout, the articles that didn't jump pages and the moronic full-color sidebars. "Great," I thought as I trash-canned the thing. "Just what the Lord's people in America need—a sanctified McPaper.")

Can't a religious impulse that has spawned things like *Pilgrim's Progress* and the works of Bach and the sermons of Jonathan Edwards and the hymns of Fanny Crosby and the film version of *The Hiding Place*—the only adequate, let alone strange and wonderful, "Christian" movie I've ever seen—get beyond pouring itself into preexisting molds (and generally disturbingly shallow molds at that)?

Wait a minute. I see that hand. Yes, sir. Yes, you in the back. Huh? What's the question? Aren't I gratuitously slamming works that are valuable precisely *because* they are derivative—works that, by virtue of reaching an audience already attuned to so-called shallow cultural molds, receive a hearing on their own terms and thereby enjoy the capacity to *lead people to Christ?* Doesn't an Amy Grant or a CBN or a *Christianity Today* (especially the newsy part that employs graphics just like those that *Time* magazine uses!) or an Aerobics for Jesus workout tape deserve our support and adulation exactly to the extent that it is a popular phenomenon, but does what it does to the glory of God?

Ummm . . . no, they don't. But thanks for getting us to the nub of the issue. See, the real problem with Christian media is not just low expectations or cheap mimicry. The real problem is the confusion of aims. Art (or even its humble cousin, craftsmanship) is one thing. Evangelization (or even its stepdaughter, edification) is largely another thing.

Both of them are good, and both of them are necessary, and at profound and subtle levels they may even intersect. (Art may evangelize—that is, embody the gospel—and evangelism may be artistic—that is, embody laudatory aesthetic designs.)

I have no quarrel with Christian media that forthrightly bear witness to Jesus Christ and seek to inculcate deeper devotion and discipleship, just as I have no quarrel with the plays of Aristophanes, Beethoven's Sixth Symphony, Picasso's *Guernica* or Joyce's *Dubliners*.

My quarrel comes with the product that seeks unearned to have it both ways—specifically, evangelization in the guise of, but without the merits of, art or craftsmanship. Dumb movies or songs or cabaret theater or sitcoms or pamphlets cannot be excused their dumbness because they invoke the Lord.

They may be (though in the end, I doubt it) an effective outreach or reinforcement on the part of the Christian community, but they ain't satisfactory comedy or rock or journalism or whatever they purport to be unless they meet the standards of comedy/rock/journalism that are inherent to the field in question—that is, unless they are funny, moving or accurate.

Christians whine because their books and records and movies sell a million copies or tickets but don't show up on the *New*

York Times bestseller lists or the *Billboard* Hot One Hundred
or the *Variety* tally of box-office grosses, or don't get reviewed
on "Entertainment Tonight" or plugged on "The Tonight
Show." All Rodney Dangerfield-like, in short, they don't get no
respect.

There is some—limited—legitimate cause for complaint here.
But there is also the taint of special pleading. Christian writers
or singers or directors want the built-in audience they can get
by working through a Word or a Sparrow or a Billy Graham
Films, and they seek to cash in on the identification they can
receive by directing their efforts to a segment of the society that
shares their presuppositions (and that will overlook their aesthetic shortcomings 'cause they're praisin' the Lord), but they
also want the benefits that will accrue solely from competing in
the open market of talent and ideas.

They want, essentially, to labor in the vineyards of evangelization (again, a noble enough venture) but to reap the harvest
that is only to be found in the vineyards of art.

(The counterargument to this analysis is that the open market
for talent and ideas, the set of criteria that determine artfulness,
are controlled by media types who are themselves so thoroughly
secularized that they ignore out of hand anything submitted to
them by the religious community. Again, there are grounds for
the justification of this hypothesis, but only narrow ones. Most-
ly, and increasingly, the networks, the film studios, the publishing world, the media conglomerates are profit-driven and hun-
gry for successful products. Secularized they may be. Blind to
the offerings that will garner them prestige and a pile of bucks
they aren't. Market forces and a thirst for quality will unsecu-
larize them in a hurry if there's genius on the block.)

A constructive thought to close. If there is a direction in

which Christian media need to go, I think it is to be found in an analogy to the biblical injunction that whosoever loses his life will find it. If you aspire to evangelize, then fine. Evangelize. If you aspire, on the other hand, to incarnate Christian truths in artistic or broadly commercial forms, then you will have, metaphorically, to surrender the norms of proclamation, take up the norms of creation and figure that the allegiances you have formed spiritually will shine through the designs you have plotted artistically. Write (sing, paint, dance) boldly—and trust God.

10
How to Keep Discipleship from Dying

Truth #10: You choose a church like you choose a spouse—it's a long-term commitment.

I would like to be Czar of the Universe.

No, I take that back. I'd like to be Shah of the Universe. It's easier to spell.

Unlike most people, however, I harbor this desire for Absolute Rule by Divine Right for only the best and noblest of reasons. I have no lust for unchecked power, no thirst for repression and cruelty, no grand designs for social engineering schemes that would alter anthropological destiny.

There are just some minor changes I would like to make for the benefit of humanity at large, and I would like to be able to make them quickly and completely with no red tape and no whining about civil liberties.

I'd like the authority to forbid fast-food counter attendants from asking, "Would you like fries with that?" when I've com-

pleted my order and intentionally left out fries. I'd like the
ability to prevent by fiat the showing of any more "M*A*S*H"
reruns. I'd like to be able to kick my ball out of the woods on
absurdly narrow fairways without having to take a two-stroke
penalty. (I'd let everyone.)

And I wouldn't at all mind a crack at producing the Academy
Awards and keeping them to a two-hour limit. No, this time,
really, I'd do it. No production numbers featuring twentyish
actors, all technical awards given off-camera, and no presenters
giving speeches beginning, "The film editor's magic is unseen,
but without it . . ." I could make it stick. I'm Shah, remember?

Oh, and one last regulatory fantasy. This one might be a little
stickier insofar as it violates the free-exercise-of-religion clause
of the U.S. Constitution, but bear with me. I'm sure we could
work something out.

Here's Shah Karl's primo new rule: You pick a church like
you pick a spouse. It's for life. Divorce or annulment from the
fellowship of your choice is technically possible but, like de-
enlisting from the Armed Forces at will or winning the lottery
when it goes over twenty mill and every pinhead in the state is
playing, largely theoretical.

Because here's the deal: Six months into my first pastorate,
it's beginning to strike me that the greatest strength of American
Christianity—the principle of voluntary association—may also
be what sounds like the death knell for serious discipleship in
this country.

This is not sour grapes because the flock I shepherd is losing
sheep. Matter of fact, worship attendance at Zion Community
Church has risen marginally since I set up shop. I'm not, however, vain or naive enough to think that the bolstering of our
body has to do with my pulpit pyrotechnics or my winsome

personality as much as it has to do with the natural curiosity that inevitably attends the arrival of a new dog-and-pony show on the ecclesiastical circuit.

Or worse. Several parishioners have already confided in me, in beguiling, just-between-you-and-me-and-the-lamppost tones, that they had registered their disapproval of my (generally popular) predecessor or his interim replacement by staying away from church the last year or so. Me, however, they insinuate, they see possibilities in. They've postponed jumping membership long enough to "give me a chance." (For "give me a chance," substitute the words "see the continued existence of the food pantry through their eyes" or "sermonize on hot issues to their liking.") These "wait and see" congregants constitute a small but significant fraction of the total membership of the church, and their ranks, I'm sure, will swell with time. It's the nature of the religious landscape. The "every-believer-a-theologian" hum of American Christianity has produced an atmosphere in which commitment to a spiritual community has taken fourth or fifth (eighth or twenty-third) place to private prerogatives and personal perceptions of the faith.

Why, after all, hang around the church when conflict flares, as it inevitably does anyplace where ultimate issues are on the line? Why not move along instead to the next congregation on the block? Or form your own congregation? Or best of all, form your own denomination?

(This latter practice, I've noticed, is particularly favored among Baptists. Cheesed off at the pastor or deacons at the local Hardshell Double-Dipped Entirely Sanctified Primitive Baptist Church? You'll show them. You'll form the Hardshell Double-Dipped Entirely Sanctified Primitive *Bell-Ringing* Baptist Church . . . if that name isn't taken.)

Lost is any sense that pledging oneself and one's fortunes to a particular house of worship is a particularly binding act. Fractious hostility is a given in our culture.

So, for that matter, is mobility. Several families have moved on from Zion Community and two have moved in since I've arrived. Reasons for the above-mentioned displacements have included vocational transfers, loyalty to family, need for a nicer climate, a yen for better schools and sheer restlessness.

Would it be totally out of line to suggest that loyalty to the fellowship into which God has led one should at least be a factor in the game of Relocation Roulette? Am I mad to think that in considering a move, a family unit might just ask itself, "Should our ties to our faith community be a factor in our consideration of the future?"

Time and proximity to fellow believers are crucial and interdependent dimensions in the attainment of Christian maturity. Weathering crises, sharing joys, working out dilemmas, evolving new understandings of the faith together, hanging in with one another when it's fun and when it's just duty—these are the most precious gifts the saints give to each other. Paul could've taken the occasion of any one of his ugly run-ins with First Christian Jerusalem to dissociate himself from the Mother Church on the basis of doctrinal differences or of his calling as an itinerant evangelist. Instead, he maintained his association with them, to the point of making himself Traveling Chair of their Stewardship Campaign, Widows and Orphans Division.

Which brings us to an interesting permutation of Shah Karl's Till Death or Denominational Merger Do Us Part Edict. "Would Pastor Karl," you cynically ask, "extend his church-hopping ban to cover ministers?" You bet your lace booties I would.

A seasoned minister, writing in a pastoral journal I picked up a few weeks ago, offered the following succinct advice: Always keep a letter of resignation in your desk, and never be afraid to pull it out.

Most clergy, the argument ran, are too afraid of making The Big Exit. Congregations play on this insecurity and push their leaders into situations that are professionally untenable. The remedy is a readiness and willingness on the part of Christian workers to pack up and get out of Dodge.

Perhaps when I've logged enough years of experience, I will find this to be sage advice. Right now, I find it to be positively pernicious—bilge of the highest order. Far from being the appropriate nostrum for parish recalcitrance, I find pastors' eagerness to fold their hands and shuffle their résumés to be utterly detrimental to the health of the church at large.

Apart from being lousy modeling on the issues already raised, this sort of "Keep Moving So They Can't Draw A Bead On You" behavior shows a gross misunderstanding of the nature of spiritual leadership.

Here's the drill. You start as pastor of a little church, move into an associate role at a bigger church, take a senior position at a still bigger church and then, if you've played the game well and kept your nose clean, end your career as head honcho of First Denominational in a good-sized city or affluent suburb. An increase in pay, perks and prestige at each stop is the goal. Recognize it? Sure. It's the old career ladder.

The question is, what does the old career ladder have to do with a calling to spiritual servanthood? Yes, I know that "church" is (among other things) an institution and that "clergy" is (among other things) a vocation. But church and clergy function—or should—only partly like other institutions

and vocations. The rules covering each have their own particular bumps and curves, and professionalized models of advancement that cover doctors and store managers and advertis-
ing executives don't necessarily hold for ministers.

Nineteenth-century German church leader Friedrich von Bo-
delschwingh developed a keen appreciation for the true nature
of pastoral practice, probably out of overcompensation for
growing up with an unpronounceable name. "I beg you," he
wrote to a ministerial colleague starting out at a church in Dort-
mund, "not to look upon [your church] as a stepping stone, but
rather say: Here I shall stay as long as it pleases God; if it be
His will, until I die. Look upon every child, your confirmands,
every member of your congregation as if you have to give account for every soul on the day of the Lord Jesus. Every day
commit all of these human souls from the worst and weakest
of hands—namely, your own—into the best and strongest of
hands. Then you will be able to carry on your ministry not only
without care, but also with joy overflowing and joyful hope."

This I propose to do for the souls who have been entrusted
to my care . . . if the little suckers will only stand still long
enough.

11
The Great Color-Scheme Schism

Truth #11: At your average church, it's easier to introduce a fourth person into the Trinity than to introduce a new carpet pattern into the nave.

After three years of tackling theological questions in seminary, I was ready (or so I thought) to enter the fray of parish life. The foundations of salvation, the charismatic gifts, the nature of sin, the intricacies of moral law—I was prepared to address them all, from pulpit and lectern, in the churning crucible of congregational controversy.

And here I am, enmeshed now in the first imbroglio of my fledgling pastorate. The Battle for the Bible is on in earnest. Where, you're eagerly poised to learn (does religious voyeurism come naturally to believers, or is it an endowment of the Spirit at baptism?), are the lines of dispute being drawn at the once-placid Zion Community Church? Are we talking plenary verbal inspiration vs. vague canons of infallibility? Who is disputing the authority of God's Word, and how are the hairs being split?

What precisely are the doctrinal issues at stake?

Try glossy crimson versus subdued earth tones.

Maybe someday we'll get down to a real donnybrook over what is going on between the covers of Holy Writ. For today, it is the covers themselves that are fragmenting the unity of the body of the faithful.

We're talking color schemes here, folks.

The Altar Guild took it upon themselves to invest in a new set of pew Bibles. It took them fifteen minutes to settle on an acceptable English translation (NIV with eight full-color plates; International Bible Society catalog number 19-8423). It has taken two weeks, and may carry on through the better part of Advent, for them to agree on an acceptable shade for the bindings.

Seems that the building renovation task force—a wholly owned subsidiary of the Board of Trustees—wants to repaint the sanctuary walls using a desert Southwest motif (the prospect of a buffalo skull under the Communion table is particularly promising), and Elyse Armitage declared a holy war when she found out that her compatriots among the worship planners were set to proceed with the acquisition of primary religious texts in primary decorator hues.

Laugh all you want. The Parish Board has been held hostage by the squabble. The Altar Guild almost *bought* the beige Bibles, for God's sake (actually, not especially for God's sake), but once they decided to go ahead with red, they refused to have their territorial integrity encroached upon. The chain of command is at stake. The church constitution has been invoked. Names have been called—ugly, schismatic names like "color-blind" and "tasteless."

What's a pastor to do?

This pastor, so fresh out of seminary, is responding theolog-ically. The whole brouhaha has driven me to formulate Beck's First Axiom of Ministry, to wit: "At your average American church, it is easier to introduce a fourth person into the Trinity than it is to introduce a new carpet pattern into the nave."

This observation is less flippant than it appears. It gets to the heart of the garden-variety layperson's spiritual self-perception.

Missouri-Synod Lutherans and Southern Baptists (make that any Baptists) aside, most parishioners feel themselves to be out of their depth in expressing doctrinal preferences. As long as they're not confronted with flaming heresies (questioning the divinity of Christ, assailing the omnipotence of the Almighty, extending morning worship past the opening kickoff), they be-tray a deep-seated insecurity in voicing opinions on the kinds of debates over which saints of earlier generations would have gleefully started shooting wars and inquisitions and building-ownership proxy fights. Good old Yankee pragmatism has a more tenacious grip on most North American Christians than centuries of religious contentiousness would have us believe.

You preach it, padre, and we'll swallow it, so long as it isn't too obviously *outré* and doesn't flagrantly flout some Affirma-tion of Faith that we've been reading responsively in morning worship since we were chartered.

At the same time, these same congregants are deeply invested in the fellowship to which they belong. They want to feel that they control the destiny of their church. Where, then, are their needs for ownership manifested? In matters palpable and visible. I may not know double predestination from Dutch cheese, but I do know ugly landscaping when I see it. Multiple-source the-ories or not are all the same to me, but you start rehanging the pictures in the Pastor's Gallery and you've got yourself a brawl.

Oddly enough, my reaction to all this fuss over all the wrong issues falls somewhere short of abject despair. Sure, I'd like the members of my flock to take the tenets of their faith more seriously and peripherals of sanctuary design less so. But I'm working toward both ends.

After all, I've discovered that I'm a concrete kind of guy myself. I confess, for example, to a love for office supplies. Office supplies are pure and attractive and perfectly functional and in their humble usefulness may be one of the few elements of creation left untouched by the Fall (except for White-Out, which is a direct result of the Fall).

An endless supply of little yellow Post-It notes makes me *feel* more like a professional minister than my ordination did. Slight the tangible? Not this clergy drone. I consider my insistence on the installation of little kick-down, rubber-tipped doorstoppers at all church entrances to be one of the major contributions I've made so far in my brief tenure at Zion.

OK, so it doesn't rank in importance with the eradication of world hunger or a major evangelistic initiative, but it helps the older members get in and out during the winter and, as uses of time and energy go, it beats the tar out of, say, passing another trenchant denominational resolution proclaiming "War is bad" or starting yet another new committee for adding "creative elements" to worship.

I'm beginning to think that the first rule of pastoral practice, as of medical practice, is "First, do no harm," and I've already learned not to sniff at the most modest of accomplishments, especially if those accomplishments give parishioners pride in the exercise of talents that they had hitherto thought were less "spiritual" than the ability to construct a sermon or frame a policy statement.

(You don't think that I attached the doorstoppers myself, do you? I said I was concrete, not mechanical. In a recent survey, I was named the twenty-eighth least handy person in America. It took six months of patient coaching by automotive experts before I could muster the confidence to use a self-serve gas pump, and for the safety of all concerned I still have my secretary sharpen all my pencils for me.)

Beyond all this, there are issues of sacramentalism at stake here. We Protestants tend to lag behind our Catholic and Orthodox and Episcopalian (at least the ones who are closet Catholics) brethren and, um, sistren when it comes to appreciating that the same God who chose to work first through an identifiable nation and then, supremely, through an identifiable Person may indeed choose to meet his children in a special sense at special times through elements of his creation. Those of us who reject a high-church stance for all the right reasons sometimes fail to appreciate the kernels of truth that are to be found in taking the principle of incarnation seriously. Whizzes at experiencing the Lord's transcendence, we sometimes end up as dunces of divine immanence.

None of this is to suggest that it counts a spiritual groatsworth whether the Word of God is presented in trappings scarlet or off-white, or Scotch plaid with paisley ribbon markers for that matter. What I'm contending is that an indifference to the surroundings in which worship takes place is not necessarily the mark of a perfected piety.

Show me a church that places no stake in its environment, and I'll show you a church that places precious little stake in what goes on in that environment. I'll put up with sentimental attachment to the bricks and mortar that house God's people if (but only if) that investment evinces a perhaps otherwise inarticulable longing for God.

Uh-oh. End of meditation. Elyse Armitage on line one. Negotiation time. I wonder what a Santa Fe-ish sort of ocher would do for her?

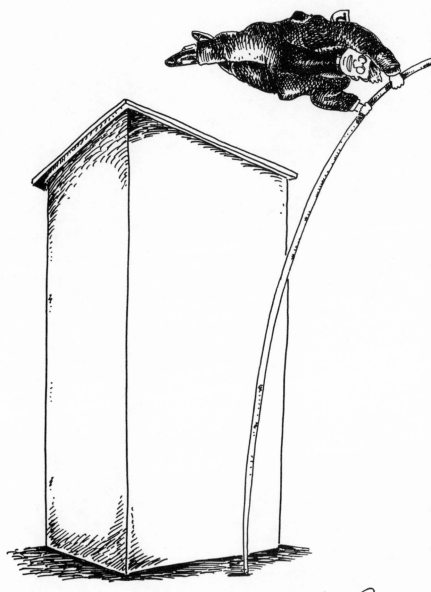

12
Why Preaching Will Never Be an Olympic Event

Truth #12: Sermons aren't supposed to be enduring literary contributions, just Dixie cups bearing living water to parched people.

I have not yet ceased to marvel at the sheer goofiness of 30 to 40 percent of the drivel that arrives across the minister's desk via the U.S. Postal Service.

Most of the really crass stuff—the breathless prospectuses from Christian custom-hot-tub-builders (superfluous in any event . . . Zion Community Church has a heated baptistery); the canned prayers I'm admonished to use in the church bulletin on the National Road Safety Sabbath (wasn't that originally celebrated the week after the Festival of Tabernacles on the Israelite liturgical calendar?); the appeals to join other right-thinking Christians in supporting God's clear scriptural mandate opposing House Bill 489 (a measure making date-nut bread the Official Baked Good of several U.S. protectorates)—all of these I accept as misguided but well-meaning gifts to brighten my day with laughter.

Some of the letters I receive, however, are more subtly exasperating. At first glance, they actually appear not to be boneheaded, and so I lose a fraction of my day reading them, often for six to eight minutes, before my stupidity alarm finally buzzes and I feed my wastepaper basket.

Here's an example from this latter category. I recently received a letterette (computer-addressed, as opposed to a real letter) announcing a National Sermon Contest and soliciting my entry in same.

In ascertaining that Ed McMahon had nothing to do with this competition, I discovered that, indeed, several of the people who had loaned their endorsements to the project had written books and articles that I have read and considered to be wise.

I'm with them so far.

The rationale behind the contest is that the sermon, which was once a vital part of both public discourse in America and the enduring literary heritage of Western culture, has sunk to new depths of nonquality, nonvisibility and nonsocial esteem. As such, it has been deemed that a competition would focus attention on the genre once again and would bring back the days of Jonathan Edwards or Henry Ward Beecher or Harry Emerson Fosdick—days when powerful preaching helped shape common perceptions. That was all seeming sensible enough to me, but then *buzz, buzz, buzz,* and I snapped to, realizing that, yes, it was of course stupid after all, as much in its own way as was the advertisement for the Christian Charm School Curriculum for Godly Little Girls that I had thrown away only moments before.

You see, one must preach many, many sermons in order to begin preaching economically and well, and it takes preaching only a few sermons before one at least begins to gain a sense of what a sermon is and what it isn't. Even with my limited experience behind the pulpit, I could think of at least four reasons that the sermon contest was foolish.

Reason 1. Sermons are not—and never have been— "contributions to public discourse." (If they end up being this, it's by accident.) Sermons are God's word to their hearers, pared down to the least common denominator within their settings. The *Federalist Papers* were a contribution to public discourse. Yesterday's editorial on raising the drinking age in the state to twenty-one was a contribution to public discourse. The rude remark that the *Gazette*'s Sally Ludlow (who had helped polish off a pitcher of margaritas while at lunch with a couple of local UPI stringers) made in a stage whisper at the mayor's press conference was a contribution to public discourse, and a very valuable one.

My sermon last Sunday—although, as it happens, *did* address raising the drinking age in the state to twenty-one—was not a contribution to public discourse. It had nothing to say to the public. I had nothing to say to the public. I was saying, as best I could approximate, what I thought God wanted the eighty-seven people sitting in the pews (and the two nursery attendants who were probably not listening over the P.A. system) to hear that morning.

Reason 2. Sermons are not—and never have been—part of the "enduring literary heritage of Western culture." (If they end up being this, it's by accident.) A sermon is not a coupon eternally redeemable for a True Fact from God; it has an expiration date, and is only good at participating outlets. A sermon is a perishable vessel for precipitates of the Spirit—not Waterford crystal to be put in a display case for the admiring ages, but a Dixie cup bearing living water to a thirsty people.

I preached a very good sermon on the Beatitudes once at the church where I served while I was in seminary. But it would be something approaching a sin for me to preach it, unreconstructed, to the church that I'm serving now, because the way the "Blessed are's" applied to the former body of Christ isn't quite the same as the way they apply to the latter one. (In fact, the former body has changed some in the last year; the "Blessed are's" don't even apply there anymore in the same way they did when I first preached the sermon.) Sermons embalmed and saved for their prose content eventually begin to rot and smell bad.

Reason 3. Preaching is not—and never has been—a competitive event. It is a gift of the Spirit. If we're going to judge the products of preaching, why should we stop there? Why don't we convene a panel to make cash awards for the Year's Best Healings and Exorcisms? Why don't we establish a weekly Top 40 for prophecies? ("Moving up a big eight notches this week, here's Ezekiel Stewart with 'Judgment Against the Nations.' ") Why don't we have Disciple of the Month recognitions? ("List five deeds of love and mercy, and enclose a fifty-word explanation of why your nominee should get the nod in November.") I foresee an Olympics of Spirituality . . . the Merton Cup for Meditation . . . the Pentecost Prize for Church Growth. Then I foresee converting to Islam.

Reason 4. Even assuming that the above reasons are faulty or not cogent, and that there is no theoretical flaw in the National Sermon Contest, I note that contest rules call for manuscripts of sermons to be submitted. But preaching is not—and never has been—a textual genre. Sermons are an oral and visual medium, performance art. Videotapes I can see, even audiocassettes, but manuscripts? That's like deciding Manager of the

Year by asking the skippers of major-league division winners to send in lineup cards from extra-inning victories and transcripts of pregame pep talks.

* * *

Ach! Here comes the church secretary with today's mail. Mail—now *there's* a textual genre. Hmmm.

Dear Holders of the National Sermon Contest:

Your idea for a preaching competition, while stemming, I'm sure, from laudable motives, stinks. If you sincerely desire to aid the cause of Christ and his church, why don't you sponsor a contest for the Best Mass Mailing by a Religious Organization?

13
Happy Birthday to Jesus, Happy Birthday to Us

A Christmas Sermon
John 1:1-14

After serving his first church twelve months, the most important truth Pastor Karl had learned (or relearned) was that the God he met in Jesus Christ is faithful. At the end of the year he stepped into the pulpit to preach the following sermon. We know Pastor Karl discouraged thinking of sermons as "enduring literary contributions," but we think this is one Dixie cup that will bear water to thirsty people even outside the congregation that originally heard it.

This morning's Gospel lesson is more than just another Scripture reading. It has been said that the book of John is the "pearl of great price" in the whole Bible, and that John's prologue—chapter one, verses one through eighteen—is the "pearl of great price" in John's Gospel. St.

Augustine and St. John Chrysostom—two of the greatest minds in the early church—each claimed that these verses prove Scripture's inspiration, since no human mind could have produced anything so sublime.

I have spent the past four weeks holding forth on the meaning of Christmas, but I recognize, as we come to Christmas itself, and as we enter the portion of God's Word that more profoundly than anything ever written probes the mystery of Christmas, that only mute contemplation and welling adoration can ever truly begin to comprehend the significance of Christ's birth.

So no sermon as such this morning. Search the riches of John's opening hymn yourself. To help you do so, though, I want to share four reflections on these fourteen verses, on this one passage which announces with such eloquence a revolution in the universe.

The Word

"In the beginning was the Word, and the Word was with God, and the Word was God. . . . He was with God in the beginning."

Ever wonder what the Bible means when it talks about "the Word"? "Your Word is a lamp to my feet," sings the psalmist. "Hear the Word of the Lord!" shouts the prophet. "The Word of God is living and active. Sharper than any two-edged sword, it penetrates even to dividing soul and spirit, joints and marrow," writes the apostle. Sometimes Scripture makes it seem that God's Word is something that comes *from* God, and sometimes that it is *part of* God, and sometimes, as the Evangelist claims here, that it *is* God. We speak of what God actually said to Bible characters as God's Word, we speak of the Bible itself as God's Word, we speak of Jesus as God's Word. What *is* God's "Word" that it can be all of these things?

Well . . . what would you do if someone asked, "Who are you?" What would you do? Would you give your name? Would you state what your occupation is? Would you tell about your life? Would you give the person something that expressed your deepest self—a picture you'd painted, a song that was yours (whether you'd actually written it or not)? However you'd answer the question "Who are you?" would be your "word."

My first day as a hospital chaplain, after we'd filled out all the forms and received all the orientation, our supervisor took us to a small room, sat us down in a circle and said some of the scariest words that can ever be uttered. She said, "You each have ten minutes to tell us about yourself. Use the whole ten minutes. Say or do what you feel you need to. No one will interrupt. If you finish in three minutes, we'll sit silent for the other seven. Tell us who you are. Who wants to go first?"

It seems as if the reason that would be scary is that it's hard to fill ten minutes, and embarrassing if you blank out. But what's really threatening about an exercise like that is the invitation to share your "word," your essence, your deepest self, with strangers who may or may not like who and what you are.

Your word is how *you* show who *you* are. God's Word is how he shows who he is. God has shown us who he is by telling us—speaking either directly or through prophets. God has shown us who he is through a book—that's why we call the Bible "the Word of God." God may even show us who he is in a sermon on a Sunday morning—that's why we speak of "the preached Word." All of these are good ways for God to express himself, to manifest himself, but all of these are also ways that humans can misinterpret or misuse.

Nothing any of us ever does will ever express perfectly who we are. Only God has ever expressed perfectly who he is, and he only did that once. There was a newborn housed in a grotto in an agricultural town in the Middle East. God said, "This baby—and the man he will become—is all you ever need to know about who I am, all I have to tell you about myself. Enough words. Here is my Word."

Jesus Christ is how God answers our question, "Who are you?"

The Creation
"In the beginning was the Word. . . . Through him all things were made. . . . In him was life, and that life was the light of men. The light shines in the darkness."

"In the beginning . . ." There are two books of the Bible which start that way. One of them, obviously, is John's Gospel. The other one is Genesis.

Genesis and John begin with the same phrase. If you've got study notes in your Bible, they will probably point that out, and they will probably observe that the similar introductions are no coincidence.

What they may not go on to show is how deeply John wishes to echo Genesis. Once you get past the "in the beginnings," you see that just as the creation story speaks of light and darkness (God's first command is "Let there be light"; then "God saw that the light was good, and he separated the light from the darkness"), so do John's opening words. Just as God creates in Genesis, according to his word ("and God said . . . and God said . . . and God said . . ."), so does John's "Word" create—"without him nothing was made that has been made." And just as Yahweh's creation climaxes in life—vegetation, teeming creatures, humans, male and female—so does John tell us about the Word that "in him was life."

Why does John echo Genesis? What link is there between the primary message of the Old Testament—that God is Creator—and the primary message of the New Testament—that Jesus is Lord? How is the beginning of time connected to Christmas?

I think John's message is that Genesis is an unfinished story—that creation is still in progress. God made all things, John acknowledges, but all things are not the way God made them. God separated light from darkness, but darkness still smothers light. God created order from chaos—in the beginning—but chaos ever seeks to make a comeback. God created rocks—and we extract the stuff of weapons from them. God created plants—and we make deadly drugs from them. God gave us lakes and we foul them, children and we abuse them, societies and we pit them against each other. In the beginning God created, and in the end we desecrated. A new beginning was needed.

That's why the Christmas story can be read as a sequel to the origins story. John shows us the completion of Genesis. In the incarnation, God finishes what he started in the creation. Because he loves what he made by his Word, God sends his Word again to remake his world.

The world, obviously, is not yet remade. Because he has not yet finished what he began in Jesus Christ, God has not yet finished what he began in the beginning. But that news—that the beginning has not yet ended—is tidings of great joy for you and me. We still have time, if any of us have not done so already, to get in on the creation of the world. We still have time to receive him whose own we are. For to all who receive him, John reminds us, he gives the right to become children of God—children of new creation. Receive him, the ancient Evangelist tells us, and you will be "born of God." "He who is not busy being born," the modern songwriter correctly adds, "is busy dying."

The Light

What's wrong with this picture? John 1:6-7: "There came a man who was sent from God; his name was John. He came as a witness to testify to that light, so that through him all men might believe." Here's another one of these biblical sayings we're so familiar with that we don't recognize how odd it is. We understand what it basically means—that John was assigned by God to announce who Jesus was, point out his importance and then fade into the background, to be sort of an Ed McMahon to Jesus' Johnny Carson. But we tend to miss the strangeness here.

Look at that light streaming in through these windows. That comes from the sun.

Why would I waste my time saying a thing like that? Why would I point something out that didn't need to be pointed out, as though if I hadn't told you there was light coming in these windows, you wouldn't have known it? Why would I "bear witness to the light"? Do you see what's strange in John 1:7? Why did the Evangelist phrase the Baptist's role as he did? Why did he use a word-picture that doesn't make sense? He's already spoken of the one John testifies to as "the Word"; why not say, "John came as a witness to the Word," or stop playing around altogether and just say, "John came as a witness to Jesus"? Why talk about a "witness to the light," as though a light needed a witness?

The only time you'd need someone to point out light to you is if you had your eyes closed. And the only reason you'd walk around with your eyes closed was if you liked the dark better than the light. And can you think of any reason someone would like the darkness better than the light?

As it turns out, Jesus did think of such a reason, and I've got to admit, it makes pretty much sense. Jesus said to Nicodemus, just a couple of chapters away from where we are now, in John 3:19, "This is the verdict: Light has come into the world, but men loved darkness instead of light *because their deeds were evil.*"

Jesus doesn't think there's anything funny about the idea of "bearing witness to the light." Jesus knows that the world is full of people who *don't* see the light, people who *do* go around with their eyes closed, mole-people, shuffling around in their dark little tunnels, not wanting to see the different life they might be shown in the light of God's presence because that would hurt their eyes, and that would mean leaving their tunnels and all the precious things they've accumulated in those tunnels—bits of string, old plastic wrappers, tin-can lids, rotting chicken bones. Who could leave treasures like that to take a chance on living in the sunny warmth of a loving God?

No wonder they beheaded John the Baptist. Bearing witness to the light is not only a real task, it's a threatening one.

We've all seen those beer commercials on TV: "Don't be afraid of the dark." I don't think most of us are. I think more of us are afraid of the light. I think more of us are afraid to open our eyes and recognize the One who made us, because if we recognize him we have to respond to him, and if we respond to him we may have to change, and even if we know that change is for the better, we still fear it.

The challenge of Christmas is to see, and to see by, the light that has come into the world. There's no guarantee that you will. You have to open your eyes.

The Exchange

Whenever I talk about Christmas, or the incarnation, I tend to talk about how God became human. In studying John's prologue, I was reminded that this is only half the story. Christmas, you see, is really all about—big surprise here—exchanging gifts. John 1:14 tells us, "The Word became flesh and made his dwelling among us." The Word that was God was given something it never had before—human form. But there's something else going on here; humanity is receiving the gift of divinity at the same time, is given something that *it* has never had before. This is true in two senses.

"To those who believed in his name, he gave the right to become children of God—children born not of natural descent . . . but born of God." Have you ever thought of the meaning of Christmas that way around? Not only is God born of a human, but because of the Nativity, humans can be born of God. Not only does God participate in what we are—through faith in Jesus Christ we can participate in what God is.

There's more to this, though. Yes, by believing in Jesus Christ we can become God's children in a special way. But there is another mystery to the incarnation that Eastern Christianity— the Orthodox Church—has always been quicker to recognize than Western Christianity—Catholic and Protestant churches. Eastern theology has always insisted that just as at Christmas God's being lowers itself, humiliates itself to accommodate humanity, so at Christmas humanity as a whole is exalted, lifted up as it takes on the weight of God in its representative, Jesus Christ. By hosting God, allowing him to dwell or "tabernacle" among us as it says in John 1:14, the race of people, and all people in that race, are raised to a new status.

This is not to be confused with, say, Mormon or New Age

jabber about our being gods or becoming God. True Christian preaching has always recognized and firmly maintained the distinction between Creator and creature. To grasp at God-ness from our side was in the beginning and is still the first sin and the fountainhead of all sin. But it is a different thing to be invited by Godself to participate in God's life, and to accept that invitation.

An exchange of gifts. That's what Christmas is. God gives his Word humanity. God gives humanity himself. It is an exchange in which Jesus' maxim that it is more blessed to give than to receive is reversed. It is an exchange in which God does all the giving, and our blessing comes from receiving the One who has been given.

It is an exchange based on new births. We focus this day on the new birth in Bethlehem, and rightly so. But let's not forget that today we celebrate as well our own new birth. "We have seen his glory, the glory of the One and Only, who came down from the Father, full of grace and truth." In seeing that glory, we are touched by it. Touched by it, we are changed by it, born anew.

It is Christmas Day. Happy birthday to Jesus. Happy birthday to us.